Living with Dolls

Katherine Massey

Keep being
Creative Queen
Love
K. Mem ♡

Katherine Massey

Illustrations: KW Paint
Copyright © 2018 Katherine Whiteway

Copyright © 2018 Katherine Massey
ISBN: 978-1727466263
ISBN-13

Acknowledgements

Thank you to my husband Craig, my childhood sweetheart, my best friend, soulmate and lover, for always helping me, being my Why. Your encouragement and support throughout this has been amazing.

Thank you to my children Harry and Olivia, they have pushed me, even when I have not wanted to write, they are my gift, and I love them more than life. I hope I have done them proud, it's all I ever wanted, to be their mum.

To all my cheerleaders, friends, and friends that are family, I thank you all for your continued Love and support, Especially A Lady called Lynne Chick, who started to make me write again, her support has been immense.

Finally, to Authors & Co without them this book would not of had its wings of life, their support, has meant the world, much love to Abi and Sarah xx

Table of Contents

Dedication

I dedicate this book to My Mother who passed away of Cancer while I was in the process of writing this book. She now at last has her peace at the age of 72, February 2018.

I had grieved the loss and loneliness of not having family around me for 13 years. Why now do I grieve for a Mother that I chose to be estranged from? A Mother that put me at harm that also caused harm?

This woman was part of my life for over thirty years.

Just a child, that wanted to be loved, I knew nothing about mental health, like I know now.

Some of the things she did, should never have happened, could she of controlled that better? YES, she should have got the professional help she needed.

Do I have regrets? Some yes, did I make the right decision? Yes, I did. The decision for my children.

Rest In peace Mum x

Katherine Massey

Chapter 1 - How will I tell Him?

What are these feelings? Why am I feeling them? Why do I feel different when I look at him?

Wait! He is looking at me too, hang on let me turn around just to check it's me he is looking at, I turn back, my big brown eyes locked with his immense blue eyes, but why would he look at me?

Here I stand with my boyish frame, long skinny bruised legs, crooked teeth, greasy hair and spotty skin, my heart racing and cheeks all warm, before me was a boy with long brown hair, cheeky smile and the most piercing blue eyes.

I couldn't stop looking at him, and to my shock he didn't seem to want to look away either, until the basketball hits me clear in the head with the teacher shouting "Miss Ferneyhough" Stop day dreaming, the boy laughs, and I share a smirk.

Eleven years young we were, in high school. I loved school, it was time for normal, to be normal, feel normal.

I was in the sports hall of the high school wearing my red PE skirt and white knee-high socks and my black pumps, I loved school uniform, it made me feel the same as everyone else.

I tried my hardest to fit in, you see my casual clothes were a little concerning, often made by my mother or hand me downs from my sister, or the charity shop.

I started to realise I was different to my friendship group.

Little did I know that, that boy across the sports hall, the one that caught my eye with feelings I had never felt before that boy would become my reason why!

I started high school as you do with your primary friends. I found it quite easy to make friends as I would always try and make people laugh, by being the class clown. I hid what was underneath very well.

That boy, he too was the class clown, always in trouble standing outside the headmaster's office nearly every day.

I would walk past on purpose just, so I could see him, another glance shared another smile, all warm inside I felt when I saw him.

His friendship group were similar to him, long hair, heavy metal t-shirts under their school shirts. He would always wear a cap, either black or red, back to front, I think I liked him more because he was different, perhaps he was like me.

But deep deep down I knew nothing would come of this, it can't, I can't let it!

I had a very unusual surname, it was Ferneyhough. Whenever the teacher shouted it out in class they would always get in wrong, it became the joke at register time, and all the other kids would call me Furry Hole, just to make fun.

I would laugh along it didn't seem to bother me, I never took things to heart or was shocked at anything, you see comparing this to home life it was a walk in the park.
I began to become friends with a large circle of girls all from different schools, all thrown together in the same high school.

Two of the girls I became very friendly with, they sort of took me under their wing, I always felt safe and good in their company. I thought this is what it feels like to have a best friend.

They would invite me round to their homes for tea or just to hang around, I never told them I was not allowed, I went anyway, I told my mother I was staying behind for extra lessons, just so I could go.

I could never invite them to my house, the funny thing is they never asked, I look back now and I wonder if they knew. I remember sitting in their home and their mums would be so busy cleaning away as they got in from work.

Putting the tea on, chatting to their dads, asking the kids about their day, and making me feel ever so welcome.

But again, I would lie, "does your mum know you're here Katherine?" I would always say yes, even when looking at them in the eye.

I had been taught very well to lie! Their homes were so different just the smell alone, and the decoration, very, very different to where I lived.

A memory I have, which has stayed with me is asking one of my friends "*How often does your mum go into hospital?*"

They just laughed and said, *"don't be silly Katherine, why would you ask that our mum is not ill, that's the only reason you go into hospital and to have a baby"*, and they carried on laughing and laughing, so me being me I laughed too, and said it was a joke.

On the way home, walking by myself, I was soon realising that I was so different, my mother was different, my home was different, why???

That boy from the sports hall, his name was Craig Julian, I always found this funny, me with the name Ferneyhough aka Furry Hole, and him with what I thought was a girl's name.

I would laugh to him about it and make fun of him because I liked him so much. He said it's Spanish, my nan is Spanish this is why I got the middle name.

I would still make fun, he would then trip me up in the corridor and laugh at me with his mates, but again I didn't seem to mind. I liked it, I liked the attention this boy seemed to want to give me.

I would lay in bed at home and dream of him, I couldn't wait to get to school the next day just to see him, to see his gorgeous brown face, big lips and them there eyes. I knew then I wanted him to be my boyfriend, but alas I sigh, I knew this could not be, it wouldn't happen.

There were a lot of girls and they were all prettier than me. All of them were getting their periods and they all had big boobs, me nope I was still waiting. Another boy would call me the ironing board for being so flat chested.

Craig would flirt with all the other girls, even kissing many of them. Why did I still feel this way about him, what did he have that no other boy had?

I wanted him and him alone, I was scared and felt so alone, I wanted him to kiss me, I knew what I was doing, I was protecting him from me, he couldn't know, he just couldn't.

We would walk home in a large group from school, everyone eventually going their separate routes for their houses. I would tend to run, I loved to run I was so fast, I would sometimes imagine I could fly, I felt the faster I ran then maybe one day I would.

Home time again, and I was just about to start running and low and behold Craig came up behind me throwing his arms over me like a bear hug, I nearly spat my Kendal mint cake out!!

I was entitled to free school meals, but all of my friendship group were not, so for me I would just stand out as the kid from the broken home with free school meals.

So, again, to fit in, I wouldn't go for them, no wonder I was painfully thin, at this point, all my friends brought money in to go to the tuck shop, to buy rubbish sweets crisps etc, so if this is what I needed to do then so be it, but I knew my mum wouldn't give me the money so how would I find it?

All I wanted was to fit in. I had been taught very well to steal, so this is what I would do. How awful when I look back now, but I was surviving, if I didn't do this I ran the risk of someone finding out about me, so I did what I knew what I was good at.

Back then people would pay the milkman or paperboy by leaving it under the bottle for the milkman to collect, I knew which neighbours left money out, so I would go and get a bit from each, how I did not get caught I will never know.

At this time my mum was with a taxi driver called Dave, he would always have change on him, he would carry a black coin dispenser and leave it on top of the fridge at home.

So again I would steal from this, just a little so he wouldn't notice, just enough for crisps and a drink just to get by and FIT IN!!!

Craig still had me in that bear hug, I wanted to be hugged forever, but part of me wanted to run and hide too, so confused, what to do???

He pulled me closer, I knew what was about to happen this was going to be our very first kiss, our chests against each other, the cold breeze running through our hair, our lips were cold, noses too, he went for it.

I didn't pull away, but stopped it quickly, and do you know what I said to him? "*Gosh you smell of cheese and onion crisps*" oh my good god, why on earth would those words come out of my mouth?

This is the boy I had been longing for, what a complete and utter cock I was being, but you see this was my coping mechanism to joke around, especially when I was nervous.

Craig just walked off, not the response he was looking for at all, I just sank to the floor and sat on the kerb, my head in my knees crying, why am I like this, why can't I let him in, why?

The mask I wore was very good, hiding my true emotions, talking of masks, I would always wear a full face of make-up, the girls would say it will give you more spots why not wear it?

But they did not know I was taught to wear makeup from the age of 3, my mother said we need to make this a habit to look our best at all times, for our men.

Back then little did I understand, her favourite words to me were "*you look pretty with makeup on Katherine* " So I quickly thought that without it I didn't, so not a day went by that I didn't have my red lips and foundation on, crazy hey!

She taught me to never let myself go, and to be fair I did feel more confident wearing it, still to this day it will be very rare to see me without any makeup on, still hiding behind it somewhat.

Will Craig ever want to know me now after a stupid thing I said? With a heavy heart I thought not, but to my amazement he did. Craig would find any way to get close to me, we were so young, could this be love? I just don't know, do any of us know what love is?

My mum would tell me she loved me, but I just thought if this is love then I don't want it. Would I ever let anyone love me? I felt I wanted to, but my god how hard it is.

Time passed, and Craig and I were getting closer all the time, he invited me around to his house, I wasn't sure what to expect but I wanted to go.

On first arrival again a different house to mine, on a private estate, he had a driveway and a garage and a car, oh no this boy is a posh boy, I thought to myself, his parents will hate me.

Their garden was all very well maintained, with a large pampas grass growing in the middle of the lawn.

Craig pulled one of the grasses out and started to chase me with it, we were laughing I had never felt so happy. I didn't want these feelings to end I didn't want to go back to my home, I just wanted to stay right here right now.

Craig's mum started to shout, "*put them there pampas grass down stop wrecking my garden Craig!*" This was to be my first meeting of the boy's mother. I did not know what to expect, Craig introduced me as Katherine, his elbow nudged me to say something, but I just froze I was so nervous.

He went on to say she is my girlfriend, oh my days GIRLFRIEND, I was shouting this inside my head, you haven't even asked me out, how would you just think I would be your girlfriend why would he take this for granted? But the whole truth of it was I was made up, oh my, me with a boyfriend, no-one could know though, it had to be our secret.

His mum was so tiny and his dad too, it really shocked me how small they were, his mum and dad still lived together in the same house, for me this was a little strange.
His mum had short blonde hair all spikey and coming onto her face, very dark skin and amazing long eyelashes.

Craig just looked like her, she was very attractive, she looked me up and down and again I said nothing, to me I thought she could sense I was different, I bet she hated me already.

His dad was there, long dark hair, dark skin and a warm smile, bit of a joker. He looked at Craig and said, "*you bringing your girlfriend in or not?*" and laughed as he opened the door and went inside, I liked him already.

I stepped inside Craig's home, there was very thick carpet my feet sank into it, it was warm and bright, with two amazing large dogs.

I could smell cooking, I could hear laughter from his siblings, sniggering because Craig had brought a girl home.

There was a wooden rail which ran the length of the room and wallpaper.
In contrast, my home was very cold, hardly carpeted, it was so bare, and no wallpaper but big drawings on the wall of a large sunset and black tree that my mother had drawn.

We had many odd things in my house, I stood there in this boys home, my heart racing looking at everything, our lives were completely different. I was different, this boy, why would he want me once he knew?

I then shook my head, I thought it's ok he will never know, I can do this, I can keep it all from him, I am falling for him, he was falling for me, why oh why did life have to be so complicated?

His parents don't want their son with the odd girl from the council estate with the mad mum, he can never KNOW, what lies behind the door of 55, my home.

It was here the day I had been dreading, but I couldn't put it off any longer, the day Craig said let me walk you home see where you live?

I would always joke with him trying to keep it from him and say it's ok, I will walk you home, I am of course the modern girl don't you know?

He would laugh and agree, but this one day he was not taking no for an answer, he even said are you ashamed of me Katherine?

I remember looking at him plain as day in the eyes, thinking Craig I am trying to protect you. Oh my good god I am so not ashamed of you the total opposite.

I wish he could read my eyes, I wish I could tell him, but I could not risk losing something, someone that had come into my life and given me happiness and hope, I had to think fast and fast is exactly what I did.

My sister had just moved out and was renting a room in a private house, I used to beg her to take me with her, but she couldn't, the house was in the next street to where I lived, so this, you see was my plan.

Craig was laughing as he walked me home we were hand in hand, stopping to kiss and cuddle, it was just perfect.

Craig leaned in and grabbed a rope like necklace that was around my neck, pulling it out of my jumper, I tried to stop him, but it was too late, there it lay on my chest a large silver whistle.

Again, Craig laughed and said "*why do you wear such a thing?*" So yet again, think quick Katherine and more lies were going to come out of my mouth. I just quickly said "*oh it's for my dog, I wear it so I don't lose it*", luckily for me he bought the lie, and said "*ok... what kind of dog do you have?*"

I was relieved because I actually did have a dog called Chelsea, a lovely white rough haired Jack Russell, Craig laughed and said *"that's not a dog, that is a rat.... ha ha"*. I think because he had Rottweiler's any other dog didn't compare, but my thoughts were its took him off the whole whistle thing.

The truth was my mother made me wear the whistle while I was not with her, she would always tell me I would get attacked whilst out and this would protect me like an SOS noise I suppose.

The whistle was used for different things too, as a punishment for being late, I was never late, but I knew today of all days I was going to be, but for that moment in time I was happy, I didn't care. I would take the punishment once home, but for now I am going to grab this happiness with both hands and run with it and that is exactly what I did.

Lying as I mentioned before came easy, but for some reason it felt so wrong lying to Craig, I wanted to share everything with him, but I just couldn't, my heart was so heavy, my feelings were beginning to get real.

I felt so strong about him and I could tell he felt the same, but here I go with the lies, I didn't know how or when it would end. I had just been so used to surviving that this at the time seemed like the natural thing to do.

We were getting closer and closer on our walk home, to what was to be my sister's home, I turned to Craig and said, "*this is me this is where I live*" His reply was "*is your mum and dad home shall I meet them?*" Again, a quick response of more lies "*no it's ok they are both at work*"

There we both stood outside my sisters rented place, I was thinking jeez I don't even live here ...think fast Katherine, I said "*I don't have a front door key just a back one and my mum doesn't like anyone round without her there is that ok?*" His reply thank god, "*Of course I can come in some other time to meet them*"

My sister's house looked like Craig's. I was so pleased I had thought of it, Craig was watching me walk onto the drive to head round the back, I didn't even know if my sister was in let alone any of her flatmates.

My heart racing again, I turned to him all of a glow as he raised his hand to wave goodbye. I was so hoping the gate would be open Craig was still there looking, thank god it was.

I raced into the back and sat on the step trying to hide from any windows, I waited a good 10 minutes to check the coast was clear, I slipped around the corner, and yes he had gone.

I absolutely leg it home, I was so so late, I knew what was waiting for me back home, but I didn't seem to care. I had just been passionately kissed by a boy I had feelings for. I will take whatever is coming to me, because for that moment it was worth it.

How long can I lie for though really, how long? When he finds out the truth, my happiness will be over, he won't want me, so I will continue the only way I know and that was to survive no matter what.

Chapter 2 - "Let me take you back..1978"

1978, I was three years old and this was my first memory, forty years on and it still haunts my very soul as vivid as can be, now, as it was back then.

When I hear people say *"Oh gosh I have a memory like a sieve"* I only wish that my memory was like that, but for me it was like an elephant, I never forgot anything.

The big black cab pulling up outside my home where I lived with my mother, my dad and my sister, my other siblings had already moved away by this time, so it was just us.

You see my mother was brought up just by her mum, her dad died very young when she was only a teenager, so a difficult time to lose any parent.

My mother's brother also died young, so this affected my Nan, she was left a single parent to bring my mother up.

My Nan suffered with mental health, my mother's childhood was not the best once her father had passed, her mother turned abusive, mentally and physical. Her only hope was to marry young to get out, and that is exactly what happened.

So long before I was even thought of, my mother married at sixteen years old and had three children by the time she was nineteen, unfortunately for her the man she married turned out to be the devil himself.

What I am trying to do here is give you the reader a little background on my mother and my siblings, but what I won't be writing about is their story, that is for them to write one day and share with you, but as a reader you need to understand the depth of it, so I will go on.

With my own memories, my memoirs, my own life story, to help myself heal and to inspire others to do the same.

Where was I? oh yes, the devil!!! I was only told about him by my siblings, my mother would never talk of this at all.

My mother a very tall slim lady with bright red hair and curls, not like your pillar box red, more of an auburn but brighter, big brown eyes, large lips, she was very attractive, this is how I remember her.

Friends would call her the match, at first I thought it must be because of all the smoking she did, but then the penny dropped it was because of her build and hair colour, it often made me giggle.

With lots of freckles, quite ginger skin she was never tanned, I would look at her chest as a child, it was full of scars, deep deep scars, I often wondered what life had thrown her way, such a story or even a book she should of wrote.

I am one of five siblings we all look very different from one another, we all had different dads.

But let's get back to the first dad of my brother and sister, this was the man my mum fell in love with. He was going to save her from what I can only describe was a life of hell, but from one hell she fell straight into another kind of hell and this was the start.

When I was old enough my siblings and I would all sit round and talk about the past, I would mainly listen, I was a lot younger and it was their past and not mine, they would turn to me and say " don't worry Katherine you are the golden child you are protected, you are different nothing will happen to you we promise.

I would just stare at them with my thoughts and listen on not quite understanding what they meant by their words, but I loved them, I felt safe with them.

My poor poor brother subjected to sexual, mental and physical abuse, along with my eldest sister, by a man they thought they could trust who they should have felt safe with, and a woman our mother watching on and letting this happen and even being a part of it.

My mum would say she was so scared of this man that whatever made him happy and left her alone she would do, even if that meant using her children to give happiness then so be it.

I mentioned earlier while writing I would not delve into the deepest darkest of their abuse just a little insight, so my memoirs make sense to you...

My mother carried on with this man knowing what a monster he was to her and her two children, his children. She had left her family home to escape, she had no one to turn to not even her own mother.

To be fair my mother was only a child herself, how heart breaking being taken advantage of by yet another man. The difference being there were children involved, her children, but this didn't seem to make her find the strength to leave.

No, instead she started to have an affair with another man, a kind loving man, someone that give her hope that she had a future.

Someone who said he would take care of her, get her out of this abusive marriage. She fell pregnant to this man, with my second sister, but she was still married to her first husband.

Time went on and she was starting to show, her first husband thought it was his child, and why wouldn't he? Many times, over repeatedly raping her. Sometimes in front of the children.

Why wouldn't he think it was his? until one day when my mother's world came yet again crashing down. The first husband had found out about the affair, he had left my mum for dead on the floor, after punching all of her teeth out.

She must of lay there holding her unborn child, thinking she would lose her, while my siblings watch on terrified, as that man her first husband killed the man she loved.

My mother fought to survive, and the baby survived too, that being my sister. She was now nineteen in Manchester with three children, nowhere to turn, no home to call her own, they all ended up in a women's refuge in Liverpool and this is where my story, my memoirs begin...

My mother loved to write, how funny as I write these words into this book, knowing I do have some influence of my mother's.

Even after all the heartache she adored men, loved them. Maybe she was still searching for someone to replace the man she lost or a father figure, someone to make her safe and look after her. I really don't have the answer to this, only that she loved men and they would always come first before any child or children.

She picked up the local newspaper and inside close to the back was the find a friend page. A whole section of male and females looking for pen friends.

She started to write to a very young man who lived in Wiltshire, he was a farmer's son, he too was to become a farmer. The young man was one of three children and they all lived on their family farm.

By this time, years had passed, and my mother was now twenty-seven years old with three children. Getting by, moving about a bit, they were now all living in what was called the settlement, it was a caravan park.

Her pen friend the farmer's son, they were getting closer. This man, well boy was only eighteen years old, nearly the same age as my eldest sister, what was he searching for in an older woman with three children?

Little did he know, age had no meaning to my mother, it was just a number. She would often say, if happiness comes knocking then grab it. I still stand by this today myself.

Before you know it, there was a paper pen friend romance, and my mother, yet again, lifted her children from another school away from friends they had made. She was off to make a life in Wiltshire with the farm boy. My mother was getting married again this would be husband number three.

The farmer boy lived in a very large house, with his parents and sisters, the only boy, so his father was leaving him the lot. He was to take the big farm house, the land the animals and make a life for himself.

I can only imagine what his parents must of thought of an older woman coming into their son's life with three children in tow, with their boy so young, but my mum made him happy. What she didn't like was farm life.

She never settled there, she told her husband she wanted to leave and guess what? that's exactly what happened. This boy loved my mother dearly, and treated the children as his own family, so where she went, he went.

He gave up his life on the farm, his home, his inheritance, all for love. At last my mother had found true love, someone that would walk to the ends of the earth for her to be happy, to take her children on, provide and protect her, that farmers boy turned out to become my dad, my real dad.

They were married for a very short three years, and I was born in 1975. My dad had already had practice at being a dad with my mums three children, who were not easy and never gave him any peace.

So now in 1975 he was set to have his own child at the mere age of twenty-three. My mother was now in her thirties.

He would look at me and say I looked like the lead singer out of Hot chocolate, dark hair and skin, large lips and big brown eyes, I was the image of my mother and eldest sister.

At last my mother had her own safe secure home, with a husband that worked and provided for four children, even giving them all his surname so we were one big happy family. That was short lived.

You see my mother was a very complex character, you think she would now be at her happiest. Her children were all safe and so was she, but her mind didn't work like that, she was bored of the marriage, bored of my dad. She wanted excitement.

My mother suffered with mental health just like her mother before her. She was a manic, now called bipolar, mood shifts like you wouldn't know, highs, lows, you just never did know what was coming.

Perhaps my dad was just too safe for her, who knows I don't have the answer to this. We are back to 1978 and I am three years old, the big black taxi was outside my home, where were we all going I wondered.

There were lots of boxes outside up by the wall of our house, and plants in pots and clothes in bin bags. My mum grabbed my hand and passed me to my sister, my other siblings had already moved away by this time, so it was just me and my second eldest sister left at home.

Holding her hand, we climbed into the back seat of the taxi. I remember holding my doll that came everywhere with me, seeing my dad on his knees sobbing, crying please don't leave me don't go. I am crying too now, all confused not knowing what was happening. I wanted to get to my dad, where were we going, why wasn't he in the taxi with us, what was going on?

I waved goodbye crying, my sister held me close. You see she was only thirteen years old, and she was not crying, she was used to this, it had happened many times for her and my siblings. She brought me closer and whispered in my ear "don't worry Katherine I will look after you now."

My mother was laughing with the taxi man, I didn't understand, and then she kissed him, why was she kissing the taxi man?

We only drove to the next street, pulled up outside a red brick house with an orange front door and the number fifty five on it.

I felt cold and alone where's my daddy, where's my daddy? no one answered, no one cared, but for me my world just fell apart right there.

Was the taxi driver to be Dad number four? Still holding my sisters hand as we entered the house, it was so cold, and smelt, no carpets or curtains, where's my bed?

There was nothing, just us and the clothes we were in and the strange man from the taxi.

My sister picked me up, I wrapped my legs around her waist and snuggled into her neck with my arms tight around still holding my doll.

My mother quickly pushed my sister and told her to put me down, there are going to be a lot of changes and you two need to grow the "Fuck" up!!!

My sister did not answer back as I started to cry again shouting daddy, my mum lent over and smacked my legs till they were red until I stopped crying, my sister did nothing, but comforted me afterwards while the taxi man look on and laughed, with my mum saying bloody kids!

My sister was born as a love child, her father killed. She looked so different from me. Pale skin, black hair, small green eyes with my mums freckles. I knew she was scared of our mum, perhaps she reminded mother of her loss too much, I just don't know, but mother didn't seem to care for her, like she was just an inconvenience.

My dear dear sister had ten years with my mother prior to me being born, what had happened to this poor child for her to be terrified of a woman that was her mum?

We had a special bond, she was going to miss my dad too, he had shown her stability for the first time in her life, our worlds turned upside down, how could one woman do this to her children, again it boiled down to a man!

All I could think of is, where is my Dad and why is he not coming to rescue me?

Chapter 3 - Life Without Dad.

The days and nights were so long. Watching and waiting is what I seemed to do. Pressing my nose against the cold glass, watching the world go by from my window, but my world the one I knew and loved, where had that gone?

The cars all passed, but my Dad never appeared. Where was he? Did he know where I was? Would he ever come back?

These were all my questions I had, but there was no one there to answer them. My sister would say *"best not ask mum about your dad Katherine, it will only cause trouble"* So for her sake I never did ask.

It was like he had never existed, but I could see him when I closed my eyes at night, I could see him holding my hands, spinning me around singing ring a ring of roses a pocket full of posies, a tissue a tissue we all fall down.

I could smell him and feel his safe warm hands around me. I remembered his hands big and wide with moon shaped nails. When I opened my eyes, my reality was starting to sink in.

My mother was making the new house into a home. She seemed happier here. I would watch her lay her tablets out on the top into little piles, then she would pop the kettle on, get the same cup every morning, while the kettle was boiling she would sit at the kitchen table on a chair.

There was a cupboard above her head and a large black phone on the wall. Here she would take papers out of a packet, put the brown stuff in the paper and roll it tightly, licking the paper with her lips back and forth, until it was like a small thin sausage shape.

She would take the lighter and press down on the silver bar over and over until a flame appeared, she would light the end of the paper, and a big ball of smoke would appear.

I watched her take a deep breath in and then out again the smoke filling the room, she would be coughing but still another inhale and exhale.

The kettle clicked, she got up poured the boiling water over her tea bag, while fetching the milk from the fridge, stirring the cup back and forth, over and over, then grabbing all the pile of pills, and popping them into her mouth, throwing her head back, and sipping the hot tea, until the pills were swallowed.

This was her routine every morning, this seem to make her happy for a while, I never questioned it.

My sister would sit there rolling the paper for her and making lots and lots of the sausage stick things, all into a pile.

My mum would then open a silver tin, a square like tin with shapes on the top, all those things that made the smoke went into this tin, and that was her day set, along with a morning nap and afternoon nap.

The afternoon nap would take place in front of the fire in the best room. She called it her best room, this was the room we were not allowed in only at certain times.

She would lay on the floor because she suffered with her back, and she would sleep for one hour every afternoon, then the routine of tea making, pill popping and smoking all started again.

My room was very small with just a bed in and of course my doll's.

My mum had wallpapered one of the walls in a Victoria plum style, which was a little fairy like girl with a toadstool hat, it was purple and pink. I remember it well, I would squint my eyes in bed and make shapes of the funny wallpaper and make up songs and stories to myself.

I had matching bedding and curtains, my mum loved design and interiors, she would make this all herself on her singer sewing machine, that was in the little room.

The little room was made up of a sofa, sewing machine and big welsh dresser, lots and lots of teapots on here, ones she had collected from the charity shops, small square window with netting on overlooking the garden.

We were allowed in here more often, it was like my mums making room. We would often go to a big shop where my mum would purchase lots and lots of material to make different things, for the house or clothes for me and my sister and for herself.

She seemed really happy, she was over the moon with my bedroom, and she would make my bed as soon as I got up all straight and crisp, then that was it, I wasn't allowed to sit on the bed once it was made, not until bedtime, so I would play on the floor.

I would lean my back up against the bed to play with my dolls, mother would come in and pull me from it so she could then straighten the blankets once again, this made her happy.

There was a built in cupboard in my room, one which overhung the stairs. This was where all my clothes hung so neat and tidy, but I could fit into it. I could get right to the back behind the clothes, I would spend many an hour in the cupboard, playing, with my imaginary friends and dolls.

My mum would come up with her tape measure around her neck and pins in her mouth just resting on her lips. She would strip me down to my vest and knickers and be measuring me, spinning me around, popping fabric around me, placing the pins out of her mouth onto the fabric where she wanted them to go.

She would then take the material and run down to her sewing machine, and before you knew it I had a full-on dress with matching ribbon hem and ribbon in my hair and frills on my socks.

My mum would do this often, tell me how pretty I looked, she would then put makeup on me, bright red lipstick and pink cheeks, she would stand back and say there, you look better now, just like a doll you are Katherine, my baby doll!!!

I always looked like this, hair braided into plaits or bunches, and she would cut my fringe. A big thick fringe, I remember it being heavy on my forehead and so hot, it was always crooked.

My siblings were a life she wanted to forget, so for her to have this little girl, me, that she could make all pretty and dress up. Looking back, I knew no different, it's only now as I look back as an adult what a troubled soul she was.

Using her daughter, her last baby girl, trying to make up for the mistakes she had made along the way, who knows!

It was starting to make sense to me now, why my siblings would call me the golden child, the untouched one. I was the child from the man that had never hurt her, one that had given everything to her, so why was he not here? Where is he? ...my Daddy.

The strange man from the taxi was not here anymore, my mum had now brought another man into our home, a very small man, with a big moustache, and long dark hair, dark skin, and a huge tattoo of Jesus on his back, this was husband number four.

He was a hardworking man. Who carried bricks for a living, he may have been small, but he was very strong. This man also loved my mum so much. Another man that has taken on her children, she said we can call him dad, but I never did. I had a Dad; this man was not my dad so why would I give him that title?

My mum's eyes could tell a thousand stories, I would look and see a glimpse of happiness, but you could see she was not happy. What was missing in her life? Men were giving her everything, their love, their money. She had her own home, healthy children, what would make her truly happy?

For years she had been abused, mentally, physically, sexually, why was she not grabbing onto some security even if it was to keep her children safe? I was so confused by this.

Time seemed to pass so slowly. I would watch the kids in our street playing, I would sit on the step of my front garden. We had a wall with railings on and a matching gate. Sometimes I would swing on it, it would squeak.

Everyone in the street had the same gates, all our houses looked the same, our garden was nice though another thing my mother was very good at. I would watch her plant things and change things around, this is when she was at her happiest.

All the other kids dads would be pushing them on their bikes, laughing with them. I would look up and down the street hoping my dad would come, but he never did.

I was walking down the stairs of number 55, I overheard my mother talking, she was talking about my dad! So slowly I creep back to the top of the stairs.

At the top of the stairs was a wall with wallpaper on, underneath the paper I had been using a nail to screw the plaster from the wall. I had done this over and over until eventually the screw had made a hole, like a peep hole, a hole that would let me see directly into the kitchen and listen.

All the adults would hush once I was in a room, so it was my little way of knowing what was going on, my very own peephole, hidden under the paper so my mum wouldn't find it.

There I was listening through the hole, my ear pressed firmly on the wall, my mother began to say, "*Malcolm has taken his life!*" ….Malcolm! My heart racing Malcolm was my dad. I wanted to scream, cry, anything with the emotion I was feeling, but all I could do was sit next to a hole in the wall.

I covered my mouth so I could listen some more, tears rolling down my face, my nose all snotty, then I heard, lucky for him they pumped his stomach and he still lives, but he has had a nervous breakdown and is in a Psychiatric ward...What was I hearing?

My Dad's alive, he's alive! I wiped the tears from my face and sat back towards the wall. I didn't understand what a breakdown was, all I knew was he was alive, and for me that was all that mattered.

My dad must of took the break up from my mum really bad, to want to end his life. Still feeling confused all I could think of was, he had me, why wasn't I enough for him to want to live? I am his little girl, but he chose to nearly end his life.

I didn't blame him at the time I blamed my mother. If she hadn't of had the affair, if she hadn't of left my dad we would still be a family and my dad would not be in hospital.

I couldn't tell my mum what I had heard, I wondered if I would see him. Would they take me to the hospital? That day never came, no hospital visit, no mention of him, would I ever see him again? If he wanted to end his life he probably doesn't want to see me anyway.

Heartbroken and alone, let down by so many lies.

I began to think of a life without my dad. Would I start calling my mums new husband dad? would he replace my dad? would that feel right?

So confused and hurt.

Life went on. We were off to the post office with my mum for her to collect her money. She went every Monday.

Back then you left your children outside in prams, or to play while you went and chatted to other mums, and did what you needed to do, funny hey?

I wouldn't even tie my dog up outside a shop let alone leave my child unattended, but this is years ago, where it was quite normal to do this. I was outside the post office waiting for my mum, when a car pulls up.

The man driving looks over at me, I don't recognise him. My eyes stare at his, then all I feel is another man holding me and throwing me into the back of the car, the car sped away.

I was rolling all over the place, screaming. I got myself up and knelt onto the back seat to look out of the window, all I saw was my mother screaming and crying, shouting someone has took my daughter, she then faded into the distance.

I turned around to a voice I knew, the man in the passenger seat said calmly and kindly, Katherine it's ok, and to my delight the man in the passenger seat was my Dad!

My daddy, I leapt into the front seat and wrapped my arms tightly around his neck, just looking at him. In his calm voice "*Katherine are you ok?*" I said nothing I just kept staring into his eyes, touching his face, "*my daddy came, he came to get me.*"

The other man turned out to be my eldest sister's boyfriend. They had been following my mum's movements and every Monday at 10am would be post office day, to collect her benefits. So that was the day my dad decided to take me. I couldn't have been happier.

We arrived at a row of shops with houses on top of them. There was a hairdressers. My eldest sister came running out of the salon, she held me tight and smiled, she turned to her boyfriend and my dad and they were all smiling. I was not scared at all, I wasn't even thinking about my mum. I just wanted to be with my dad.

My dad took me up a steep set of steps. It was a dark corridor and the steps were navy blue. It took me a while to reach the top with my little legs.

There was a door, my dad put the key into the door, I said "*A house in the sky?*" Dad laughed "*No Katherine it's a flat, it's our new home.*"

Dad showed me around, it seemed massive, but I was small remember so everything would seem big.

Large hallway, kitchen living room, two bedrooms, one with all glass and a door with a balcony, and a bathroom with a funny window in the roof. I loved it, but it didn't matter I just wanted to be with my dad.

Then my dad's face changed, like so different. He looked at me and stroked my hair saying *"My brown eyed girl, you give me reason to live."* But then the words I did not want to hear, *"Katherine I am going to have to take you back."* NOOOOOOOOOOO.....My heart sank, I have only just arrived, why, why?

The police were looking for a little girl that had been snatched by two strangers in a car from outside the post office, But your my dad. *"I know Katherine but no-one else knows this."*

So, with this, my dad took me to the police station. Walking down the long white corridor holding his hand so tight, I did not want to let go. There at the end was my mum, hysterical, she turned and saw us both, she snatched my hand from my dad's and looked at him with such hate, we were all crying by now, then the policeman took my dad to another room.

We left, we left my dad there. I was sobbing, I held her hand, and walked away, looking over my shoulder, but once again my dad was not there. It was just back to us again, heading back to number 55.

Wondering what had happened to my dad, but taking some comfort in the fact he did want me.

I realised now he too was a broken man. He had left all that he ever knew back on the farm with his parents and siblings, for a life of love, a love that didn't last. He too was trying to understand a woman's mind, a woman we both loved, a woman that was so confused.

He would now have to rebuild his life and hopefully find love again. I could only hope that I would be part of his new life. Just because two parents separate and divorce, they should never divorce their kids. We are not the baggage that some would refer to us as.

Let me tell you about my dad, A very hard working man, a man that went on to throw himself into work. Maybe this was to keep his mind sane, who knows. He used to be the pop man, driving the open back truck, filled with glass bottle of all your favourite fizzy pop.

My favourite and still is, is cream soda and dandelion and burdock. He went on to sit at people's houses selling insurance, then a car salesman, a far cry from life on the farm!

Some would say a work alcoholic or was this to bury his head in the sand to his real life? Answer is I don't know.

Going back to life without dad, it was something I had to get used to. There was always male traffic through number 55, no one ever replaced that man I called dad, no one.

The day came, the day my mum sat me down and actually talked to me about my dad. She went on to say, "*He has bought a hairdresser's and it has a flat on top*".

I didn't mention I had already been there the day he took me! I learnt quick on what to tell my mum and what not to tell her, funny hey? As young as I was the game of life and survival was coming easy.

"*Your dad has met someone.*" I remember the words to this day! I don't remember feeling happy for him, I remember thinking how does my mum know? and who is this other person? another person to take me away from my dad.? "*Your dad will pick you up every weekend on his day off on Sunday.*"

"You will spend the day with him and his new girlfriend."

Inside I was thinking, new girlfriend? how many has he had? what don't I know? why is everything kept from me?

I had not seen my dad since the day of the police station, so I was excited to see him, and to have him back in my life, even if I had to share him.

The car pulled up outside 55, my dad got out. I could see him walking up the path. I was dressed in something my mum had made. She had done my hair in braids, I was so excited, but couldn't show it, I didn't want to upset my mum. I showed no expression on my face not even a smile, I just kept it all inside.

The door opened, my dad stood there all tall dark and handsome. He lent down to my level, he smelt of aftershave and was clean shaven, wearing a jumper and flared jeans. My small hand touched his face, *"Daddy, Yes my Katherine, Daddy."*

To which my mum shouted *"make sure you feed her I have nothing in"*, *"Of course I will Eileen"* was his reply, the tension, I just wanted to go. I grabbed my dad's hand as he swung me up into the air, this was happiness, I was happy.

Through the squeaky gate we went. "*We are going to the fun ship Katherine.*" I had no idea what this was, I didn't even care, I was with my dad.

I had nearly forgotten about the new "girlfriend", but there she was in the car, blonde curly hair, round face and small, nothing like my mum, nothing like her at all! It was from this day forward I knew I would never have my dad to myself again.

Chapter 4 - Grandma's House

My life is going in three different directions, I am a different person in each. My first Life living with my mother, this life is full of sadness, loneliness, mania and depression.

A life where I cannot be my true self, I cannot be the child I am, I am suppressed, my emotions, reactions. I am so young, but smart enough to know what it was I had to do to make life easier living with mother.

My second life with my dad, well if you can call every Sunday a life with your dad! Picked up to spend quality time together but never on our own. I was now sharing my dad with a stranger, but I adjusted, I was good at that.

Life with Mother had lots of traffic through the house of strangers. I knew what to do, how to be, so I treated it the same, such a young life. That had already seen, heard and felt so much.

Our Sunday's were quite the same every week, that's when my dad was not working on a Sunday. I would wait as always by the window then my mum would say, he's not coming he's working, nothing changed there then.

When we did go out we visited places like the park, the local pub for crisps and a pint for my dad, and not forgetting the famous Fun Ship. This ship had a cinema on it.

We would watch the same film most weeks 'Watership Down'. I would cry every time as the song played 'Bright Eyes'. I was an emotional being when I was with my dad, either that or I used to say I was bored. Today my dad still calls me his bored little girl.

I would love to watch TV, something that didn't happen with my mum because the TV was in the best room, and we were only allowed in that in the evening if invited in.

My favourite were the Terrahawks, A-Team and Worzel Gummidge, and if nothing was on we would play the game of perfection.

My third life was life with Grandma, my Grandad too but I always called it Grandma's House.

This was my happy place, a place I could just be me, I could be that child that was inside of me, no pretending with strangers, I was safe, warm and felt like home, a real home.

Grandma's House, even writing those words fills me with such emotion, even now I have so many happy memories, happy times.

My Mother would go into hospital quite a lot, she was not sick, well not like you think she was, it's just a thing that was normal a thing that happened all the time, it was normal to me. I thought every mum did this.

Social Services were involved in our family because of this, and from the time my dad snatched me. So when the ambulance would pull up, it was coming for my mum. Any other child would be crying and sad wanting their mum to be ok, I was not that child.

My whole body would fill with excitement, my face of course would not show this. When my mum went away it was relief, a break from all the heartache and sadness. I knew I would go to my grandma's House.

Why did my dad not look after me I hear you say, guess what? He was working, so, like most parent's parents help out with the kids, it was no different, just that my grandparents lived a 5 hour drive away.

Grandma sometimes couldn't have me, so I would go to a lady from our street. A lady I called Auntie Pam, she wasn't my auntie, but we all had them, didn't we? Like a respect thing to call them Auntie. If it wasn't for her stepping up or stepping in I would have gone into foster care again, so these women quickly became my role models.

You see Mum's visits to the hospital were not an overnight stay, they could last weeks, months, never quite sure of her return, most occasions, she would discharge herself though.

My auntie lived 5 doors down from 55, she had lived there all her life with her husband and 4 children. They soon were to become my second family.

I was treated like one of their own, my Aunt became my mum's best friend, and I became best friends with her youngest son. I have so much to thank this lady for, she kept me safe, fought my corner, fed and watered me, and told me off if needed too.

When mum went into hospital and the circumstances of this made for their friendships to have a long and bumpy road.

My auntie Pam soon figured out how unwell my mum was, well her mind, and like us all was trying to understand it, and the choices she made that came with her illness.

When mum was good she was the best most caring friend you could have. Everyone would say how nice she was, even though she was known as mad Eileen. But no one knew the extent of her illness. An illness that nearly killed her several times over.

Let me tell you more about Grandma's House for the moment.

My dad would pick me up and take the long journey down to Grandma's which was in Wiltshire. His parents, my Grandma and Grandad had now sold the farm and bought a house with no stairs. I had never seen such a long flat house, with no stairs.

The bungalow, as later I found out what it was, was massive, but I was small, and everything seems big then doesn't it?
We would arrive, and I would be in my knickers and vest.

I suffered with car sickness, still do, so I had probably been sick 3 or 4 times on the way there, with the constant nag to my dad of "*Are we there yet?*" This, I am sure, was a delight for my young dad.

The bungalow had a very large entrance hall, it was big enough for a large wooden table with eight chairs all matching around it. A large long window that overlooked the garden with a row of huge trees on the front, then a small road and fields beyond.

The hallway had a long sideboard that matched the table, in one of the cupboards were board games, I remember it well. There were lots and lots of pictures and ornaments of farm animals.

The kitchen was big enough to fit another table in there. What I remember the most is that Grandma was always in it, wearing a pink or blue tabard. This was a checked-like apron that went over her head to protect her clothes. There was a front pocket with mints and tissues in.

My mother used to spend all her time in the kitchen, mainly drinking tea, rolling fags and popping pills.

Grandma would be baking, or defrosting bread in the toaster she took from the freezer. I still wonder about that, haha.

The biscuit tin, another fond memory. Full of rich tea biscuits, the top would make a noise like it had rice in it. Grandma would say it does. I remember thinking you're right, it's so you can hear if anyone is taking one.

The kitchen door was always open. There was a large utility and Granddad's workshop come garage was there. This is where the large white cat would sleep, and if I recall a tortoise shell cat called tom cat, too.

Grandma was the perfect woman to me, tending to her home, her palace, making sure Grandad was ok and all her family. The heart of the home, as they say. The rock, my role model.

The things I learnt from my time in Wiltshire, I still carry these through with me today. Past that long hall was a room. I would knock on the door and walk in.

A lady lived in there, a small lady with long, long white hair. There was a bed, a sofa and dressing table with her hair brushes on and I would brush her long hair that was by her bottom nearly, and then Grandma would pin it up into a bun.

She was my Nana Collingbourne, my Grandma's mum, she lived there in the secret room as I would call it. We were not allowed to mither her since she would be resting or watching Songs of Praise, a religious programme on the TV.

There were 3 more bedrooms and a very large bathroom with a huge deep bath at the end with steps up into it, and these had carpeting on them.

I had a bath every night at Grandma's which was a treat for sure since it was very different to home life with mum, hair washed once a week and constantly told not to use too much water.

This takes us to the large living room, not a 'best one', one you could use at any time you wanted. I loved the round porthole window in the corner and the large glass window with a door in which overlooked the rear garden and pond, with fields for views.

Again, this was very different to my house with mum. We had a garden with two outhouses. My mum had done the garden lovely to be fair, but our view was garages and the local tip.

The living room in Grandma's had a large chair in the corner, and in that large chair sat a larger than life man with a big shoe on one foot. He was bald with tufts of hair at the sides, and he would have a twinkle in his eye while chomping on a Fox's Glacier mint.

A large jar of them would be down by the side of his chair and when he stood up he was a giant (to me anyhow), over 6ft, and walked with a limp from an injury on the farm.

Rosy cheeks, a hearty laugh, this man was my Grandad. Unfortunately, Grandad lived a short life but the memories I have I will treasure forever and ever. Grandma became the glue of the family, a strong woman keeping it together even though, the man, her husband and provider, had passed.

My dad was so young to have lost his Dad. It's a loss I remember affecting us all, even though once upon a time they were my Mother's in law's. There was no love lost there at all. My grandparents hated her. Hate is a harsh word, but they really did.

I never understand my dad as to why had he left such a beautiful place and I still don't. Why did he not go back there after his heart ache, why couldn't we live there, me and him, another question left unanswered.

I would be playing in the garden of Grandma's. I remember the wheelbarrow, sitting in it, while I was pushed around, shouting 'faster, faster' to my dad.

Or the blanket that was laid onto the ground. I would sit on this and my dad would grab the ends of each corner and run with the blanket around the lawn still with me in it while holding on for dear life and laughing until I could laugh no more and eventually I would fall out of the blanket and we would both lay on the floor.

We were so, so happy and relaxed here, why could we not stay, why could we not have a life here? I dreamt that one day we would, but that day never came.

My dad would kiss my head and get in his car to go back to Wales while I would stay with Grandma. I never quite knew how long I would be here for, funny thing is I had never asked. I never got homesick, I never asked about my mum. No one mentioned her at all.

The only time she crossed my mind was that time, the dreaded time we had to go back. Back to 55, back to another life, my different life. My very, very different life. No warm baths at night, no playing in the garden, no supper in the living room. So different.

My grandma made the best supper. It was amazing, and I remember it like it was yesterday.

A small-ish table that we would sit around on the floor with my cousins. There would be sandwiches, pickles, but my all-time favourite was cheese and jam on crackers. Please don't knock this until you have tried it, ha!

Then. Bedtime. The covers smelt so fresh, the pillows all plump and the carpet all thick, a bedtime story told, and even before the end I was gone, content, safe and my tummy full.

Waking up was early was very normal for my Grandma, must be the farm life still in her. She would get up at 5am!

I would lie in bed and hear her pottering around, putting the washing on the line, making breakfast. She ran a tight ship, did Grandma. Everything done just so, like a hotel.

Breakfast wasn't just a few stale cornflakes without milk. My mother had a thing about milk, we were never allowed to use much. She hated waste, but also hated to run out of milk. Another thing that stays with me in my adulthood, I am not happy unless I have 12 pints in the fridge, I kid you not!

Anyway, Grandma's breakfast had all the cereal you could imagine, lined up in the middle of the large table in the hall with a large jug of milk, and a jug of orange juice too, toast in metal racks which were cut into triangles, butter on a plate with a butter knife, jam and marmalade.

Then would come the cooked stuff. Eggs, bacon, beans, you name it and we had it. A 5-star luxury hotel is how I would describe it to you, and this was done every single morning without fail.

We would all sit around eating and chatting, proper family life. This is what families should be like, I thought. But I only got this a few weeks at a time throughout the year, I wanted it to be forever. I would imagine it but imagine was all I could do. The time had come to head back to number 55 and my mum.

All packed up again for the long sickness drive home. I used to get so upset and I didn't want to go. This felt so much more like home. Why did we have to leave and go back to the cold, tobacco smelling house of number 55.

I never ever got to spend Christmas at Grandma's, not ever. To this day, 43 years on, I have never spent Christmas with my dad. How sad is that? Most take that for granted so please don't, it's a privilege that I have not encountered.

Christmas for me, today, as an adult is a massive big deal. I make up for all the lost memories I didn't get to have.

I sit in the back seat of the car traveling back to Wales, wondering if my mum was home what would she be like this time? Would anything have changed, would she have got the help she needed, would life turn itself around? Would there be another new friend coming into our home from the hospital? My mind would be racing, and then I would feel sick.

Before I knew it, I hear the squeaky gate of number 55. Do I run into the arms of my mother whom I had not seen for weeks, tell her all my news of Grandma's...? Nope, this never happened. I would never tell her, and she would never ask. We wouldn't even talk about her hospital visit. It was just normal.

The only thing I missed from number 55 was my dog. Well, we had lots over the years. Chip, Max, Chelsea, Bonnie and Geoffrey, the cat and some budgies that would fly round the house free. Welcome back to the madhouse, I would say under my breath... Literally.

Chapter 5 - Living with Doll's

Mum had discharged herself from hospital again, but this time it was slightly different. There was no visitor with her. My mum would meet a lot of people in hospital, people suffering just like her.

She would find that she would want to help them. Strange, really, when she was not getting the right help she needed. She would bring these complete strangers' home with her.

Some for a day, some for an overnight visit, and some would stay longer maybe lodge in the spare bedroom. Others would become her new boyfriend and she'd even marry some of them. This was the extreme of her illness.

I often thought about whether my dad thinks this is ok with all of this male traffic coming in and out of the house, but it was normal, right?

They would all be on medication just like my mum, and all of them smoked. In fact, I can't remember one person that didn't. They would smoke in the kitchen with my mum.

The house was always full of smoke but mainly in the kitchen where the food was prepared. I know, makes you feel sick, right? Not like it is nowadays where everyone smokes outside.

My mum would even smoke in bed. This would be her first rollie of the day. I remember the smell so well. As a child I must have stunk, let alone who knows what it was doing to my health.

I only have to smell a fag now or see someone smoking near a child and it makes me sick. I don't bite my tongue, either.

I would just leave my mum and her new friends to it. There was no asking if I was ok, how was Grandma's house.

I would long to hear the words '*I promise to get the help I need, Katherine. I will stop discharging myself, stop putting new men into the house*'. I never did hear those words ever.

She would tell me she loved me but how could that be love? I did not want this kind of love in my life. My dad would say he loved me, but he has left me to see me one day out of 7, so how can this be love?

My grandparents had never shown emotion like that, never said the words 'I love you', so what is love? Would I ever find out what true love was?

One love I did have in my life was the love for my dolls. Yes, dolls. Quite a normal part of life growing up, with Barbies and Sindys, really, but my special doll, my best friend in the whole wide world, was William.

My new born baby doll. He had blonde hair, blue eyes and peach skin. Well, plastic, but back then I thought he was real. I took him everywhere with me. I would even cut his hair.

I thought it would grow back, what I would be doing with scissors, cutting a doll's hair I don't know, but I must have sneaked them out of the little room, my mum's sewing room.

I would talk to William like he was real and to me he was. If I ate breakfast then so did William, if I went out, William came with me.

I can't remember why I called him William, but I loved him. He would sleep in my bed every night.

My Mother had said *'you're nearly going to high school, don't you think it's time for William to go?'*. Go where, I thought. Yes, I am nearly 11 years old playing with dolls. I did not think there was anything wrong with me doing this, but my Mother had said I needed to grow up.

I tried really hard not to play with William to keep my mum happy. I loved him, I was obsessed with a doll. So, I began to play with him in secret, keeping him in the back of my cupboard and not letting anyone see. I would still talk to him. It was like having a best friend. When no one else was around, I had William. I could tell William anything.

The day had come, I am heading to high school. Secretly, I kiss William and pop him into the cupboard.

Once the school day had ended I rushed home, ran upstairs and opened the cupboard. I had missed William so much, It sounds crazy that I am talking about a doll.

I cannot see him. I even shouted his name like he would appear and say hello, but he was not there.

Where was he, where was William? I turned around and jumped out of my skin. I did not see or hear my mum enter my bedroom.

There was no how was your first day, just *'Williams gone, time to grow up, Katherine!'* The words had floored me. I cried until no more tears came. Why William, why? That doll meant so much to me, why does anything or anyone I care about have to go? It's just not fair, I was heartbroken.

Did I scream or shout? No. I knew that I could not show my emotions like this. She hated to see me cry, but I could not hold back the tears. I wished I could grow up like she kept saying, I wished I could.

My only comfort about my day in high school was seeing that boy, the blue eyed boy with eyes just like William. Little did I know that boy would replace my love I had just lost.

My mum did things I was never quite sure of. In her heart, I suppose she was trying to help me to grow up. You see, when mum was manic, she would make things like I have mentioned in the earlier chapters.

My mum was up cycling long before it was trendy. If she was having a manic day, then there would always be something made. A pair of curtains, a new dress, or she'd cover an old chair with new fabric.

She would go to the skip, or to boot sales and charity shops. Anything she could find, she would have it looking shining and new. Unique, really. She even got a cleaning job in an antique place and she would spend her wages on an item of furniture or picture. This brought her so much happiness.

My mum's special talent was painting. Not like just decorating a room, she was basically an interior designer in her own right, but people never focused on the positives. They always focused on all the negative, myself included, far too young to recognise what was right in front of me.

She would draw a plan of the room, then, all in free hand in pencil, she would draw large murals all over the wall. People pay good money for such art these days yet hers went unnoticed by many, but it brought her joy, fag hanging out of her mouth, smoke in the air, cuppa on the side and a paint brush.

This was my mum happy. Manic mindset, an illness, but when I look back, this should have been tapped into, instead of drugging and locking her up. Why when the nurses or doctors came around did they not see that this was a talented lady with a touch of madness but, like with all madness, it borders genius, too.

The old record player would be playing in the best room, Mum singing away. One thing that stood out was a large orange sunset with a black Japanese tree hanging over it. What a beautiful mural she had drawn and painted, why didn't I see that beauty? I just went with what everyone else was saying, that she's mad.

No other mums were painting their walls. I wish I would have understood, but I was a child trying to work life out for myself and it was tough.

Her garden was also truly an amazing a piece of art in itself. She would really plough herself into working in it when her mind was manic.

On returning home one day from school, Mother was leaning on the squeaky gate waiting for me. She was all excited and had been in her manic mindset for some time now.

Her eyes all glazed and sparkling, she could hardly get her words out, *"It's not finished yet, Katherine, but come see. Katherine, I know you would love the perfect family"*. I looked at her totally confused, so deep down she knew. She knew how unhappy I was, but why was she saying this now?

She grabbed my hand and like a whirlwind I was flung into the kitchen and told to sit down, which I did instantly with no questions asked.

Normal, right? Nope, most mums would say "*how's high school been, meet any friends, learn anything new, eaten your dinner, tea is cooking*", but like I said, my Mother was not like most mums, so these things were never said.

Her illness made her focus on herself and herself alone. A very selfish illness is bad mental health, so this is why I was shocked at what was so important that she wanted me to see straight away.

Opening the little room door slowly, as she did, turning to me and smiling with such excitement in her voice and eyes. The little room the making room.

There in front of me was a woman, a man and a child. They were dressed in Victorian clothes. The woman was my mum's height, with the same colour hair. She also had big brown eyes and red lips, with her white blouse all frilled right up to the neck and long black velvet coat fastened at the waist.

The man, taller than the woman, too, was in black a suit with a white shirt, his arm and hand just resting on the woman's shoulder. Then was the child, again with big brown eyes, red lips, and kneeling in front of the man and woman while gazing at them.

I turned to my Mother. I wanted to shout, "*What the fuck*", but I knew I couldn't. This would flip her, make her angry. She looked at me and said "*Mum, Dad and Daughter*", I said "*Yes, but MUM, they are dolls*".

I remember her laughing and saying "*yes, I know they are dolls, Katherine, but now you have the perfect family that we can live with in the little room*". This was said so sanely, but I knew it was her mind in overdrive.

Are you still with me on this? I know it sounds like utter madness as a reader to read such words of a Mother making life size dolls to replace the family unit we had lost, but believe me, this was my life. I now had a life of Living with Dolls, life size dolls in wigs, in Victorian clothes, oh my fucking days!

This was real life for me. A mother so manic that she thought this was normal, manic for months. Making, doing.

I could not let anyone know, but oh no, my mother had other ideas. She rang the local newspaper to come and take pictures of the dolls she was so proud of, even sharing her story of why she had made them.

The title of the newspaper cutting, 'LIVING WITH DOLLS', sounded like a horror movie, but no, it was just life at number 55. Did the newspaper do my mum any good? Nope, it just made people think she was crazier than before.

A mother whom is meant to keep you safe, look after you. This was the opposite. We were trying to understand with no help, trying to understand how her brain functioned, trying to keep her safe and not the other way around. So, perhaps, yes, I was more grown up than my mother gave me credit for.

I knew that months of mania meant only one thing and that was that we had to be ready for an earth crashing down, that with every high comes a low, that the higher you are, the lower you fall.

Mother would not see it coming but living with it, I did. We had to be ready because these lows could be heart breaking to say the least.

I was a child trying to fit into school life, trying to understand life, searching for what love really was, clinging to the fact that I would one day find it and lead a normal life, but for now it was about keeping mum happy and safe the best I knew how to.

Picture walking into my house, number 55. On entering the squeaky gate and garden path, you're met by the most amazing pink roses, all planted and nurtured by my mother. Like I said, the garden was fantastic.

So, picture the house, the beautiful gardens, the roses around the door. It all looks so nice, so fairy-like, so pretty, so normal. Right?

Open the door to number 55, no carpet as such. So threadbare. The walls all painted in different colours done with a rag and sponge by my mother. Remember there was no YouTube or Google back then, this was all self taught.

The doors were all glossed in shiny white, stairs and banister the same. Nothing matched but crazy colours to match a crazy mindset.

Then, you enter the best room, the lounge. This is where her murals where, a TV, a record player, and sofas. Into the kitchen, all the cupboards hand painted by my mother. Trinkets everywhere from what she had collected over the years.

The little room, singer sewing machine as mentioned earlier, a welsh dresser, full of tea pots, and 3 bloody life sized dolls.

Our house was crazy to look at. Filled with stuff, mix and match, different colours, murals, dolls, but to my mum it was her life. Whatever she was feeling at the time was expressed into the house. A talented lady, so lost, but to too many just the crazy doll lady from 55.

But hey, she was my mum. Had everyone forgotten this, this crazy lady had a child in number 55. Not just paintings and dolls, there was a child. Quick to stare, snigger and say comments under your breath, point the finger at her strange ways, but who was there to help, help her deal with this illness, let alone bring a child up?

She must have felt so lonely at times, so isolated. Not only in her home, but in her mind, too. No parents to turn to, no friends as such, no family.

Is this why she turned to men so frequently? She had lots of male friends. Some would turn into relationships, some she would marry and some just passing through.

Still, no one stops to help. A world of loneliness, depression, and mania. Depression in my mums form was not just feeling down or fed up, it was a chemical imbalance in her brain, but back then the answer was to take her away in a straight jacket, pop her with others the same, drug her up until she peed herself and forgot who she was.

What could I have done as a child? No one would listen to someone who's a kid. This is why I hid everything and just tried to fit into a world that did not want to deal with the likes of my mum.

Going to school acting normal, wearing the mask. Going to my dad's, acting normal. Going to my grandma's, acting normal when inside I wanted to scream from the rooftops but no one heard my words.

I would write on tiny pieces of paper like a diary, but I could not have a diary as my mum would find it.

So instead all of my thoughts, my anger, my hurt and my loneliness were all written on bits of paper that I would hide in the floorboards, so wanting someone anyone to find them and to hear my words.

Chapter 6 - It Would Not Happen to Me

Writing a book, I must say, is the hardest decision I have made. I started to blog about real life experiences. I found writing your thoughts down really helped not only me, but others that could relate.

It was just like writing on those tiny pieces of paper all of those years ago. Now with technology, we have the power to reach a wider audience. The feedback I got from my blogs blew me away, people who were complete strangers were messaging me and telling me their stories and how I have inspired them to write too.

It has been very heartfelt and a complete learning curve for me. Finally, someone was listening to my words after all these years, and more importantly my words were helping others.

This is something I am very proud of. I knew then that it was the right time to write a book, to give you more than I could ever give you in a blog.

My Memoirs, my memories, and by doing so through a child's eyes, my eyes, I hope to inspire others, to help you have the understanding that no matter what, you are worthy of anything.

This Chapter was my most difficult to write. It's so, so hard when you have not shared some of your memories with anyone, laying it all out and bearing your soul makes you feel very vulnerable. I am used to having a big brick wall up that does not come down very often.

I am not writing to show someone in their worst light. I can only write what I know, what are my memories. Like I have stated in earlier chapters, my memory is a good one but sometimes a burden.

If you are going to understand mental health then you need to understand every side to it. I did think would I share this, my answer to myself was yes. I have been brave enough to write, so it's only fair on you, the reader, to get the whole of me.

To share my deepest and darkest memories, we are building trust as you read, and my journey is also your journey. Together in writing and reading, we can both arrive at our own destination.

So, here goes Chapter 6, it would not happen to me!

Was I the golden child that my siblings often called me? Yes. I think I was more privileged than them in a materialist kind of way.

My mother's mum had passed away. My mum, the only child after losing her brother, so it was all left to her to sort out and empty Nan's flat.

Nan's flat was in Rochdale on the 6th floor, a one bedroomed flat. We would stay here now and again with my sister and mum.

Mum would sleep on the sofa and my sister and I would sleep on the floor in Nan's room with Nan and her husband (we called him Uncle). I would watch them get a glass from the bathroom fill it with water, then place their fingers in their mouths as they pulled each set of teeth out.

The teeth would go next to their bed, just floating in the water in the glass on their bedside table. I found this very odd. My mum had false teeth, but this never happened. I had never seen her without her teeth in. She lost her teeth far too young, as I mentioned in Chapter 2.

The first time I knew her teeth were not her own was sitting on her knee as a young child and messing round her mouth. I don't know why but I pulled them out. I remember mum's face now, she was devastated and ran upstairs to sort herself out.

We never talked about it again. Can you imagine being so young and then all of a sudden you got your mum's teeth in your hand? It was only later when I was older that I learnt of how she lost them, it was so sad.

My Nan played the piano. Well, an electric keyboard that was in her lounge. She only had one lounge, kitchen, bathroom and bedroom. It was a strange place and never felt nice there, just another home that smelt funny of stale tobacco.

And grease from my uncle's hair. Another odd thing I would watch him do was fill another glass with water and add sugar to it, place his comb into it and after a while he would comb his hair with the sugar and water. It would go rock hard just like hairspray, giving him a big quiff, then he would place his teeth back in.

Nan was like mum, in looks and in ways. Very strict. She would shout at us and smack us, mum just used to let her like it was normal.

One day, she even dangled my sister over the balcony of the flat. "*I said you better be good or I will drop you*", strange lady. We had no love there. I hated going there and it was very different to Grandma's house, very different.

Anyway, she had passed away and so had my uncle. My mum was keeping all the furniture she wanted and selling bits and bobs she did not want. Everything was being brought back to number 55.

I had moved into the bigger room by then, it looked over the garden and on to the tip that was on the back of the fields. It was so big compared to the box room, it had no cupboard either.

My mum let me paint it. I painted it white and used one of my mum's stencils. I put black tulips all the way around it and I loved it. I had not realised how much I had learnt from my mum.

Mum said I could have Nan's old sofa and chair. It was only small, wooden base and arms with a floral print cushion. I was also given her black and white TV and old record player.

It was like my own little palace, I was so chuffed and felt very grown up, but I wasn't I was just a kid, who had inherited all this stuff, I did not ask for any of it. Yes looking back I did have it better than my siblings.

I was now the only child in the house living with my Mother, my siblings did not know the full extent of living with mum, looking after her. Their memories are theirs, and these are mine, I can only write my own.

I had got to a certain point in my life where I was struggling, I was struggling with my health. I was painfully thin and suffered from severe headaches, migraines, mouth ulcers, stomach and bowel problems.

If you have ever had a mouth ulcer you know how painful they are, but mine where like big craters in my mouth, they would run along my whole gum line, in my throat, under my tongue.

Mother would take me to the doctor's, he would say "*Katherine are you worrying about anything?*"

My Mum would quickly reply, "*Of course she is not worrying, what would she have to worry about?*". Looking in from the outside, what would a young girl have to worry about right!
But like the doctor and the neighbours, they never saw what went on behind the door of 55. I had anxiety, I did not know it was this back then, as I do now.

My diet was lacking in certain vitamins and my iron count was low, this is why I was put on iron tablets, that lead to constipation. I was always in chronic pain, going to the toilet was a nightmare. I remember shouting to my sister once to help me the pain was so bad.

Mother took matters into her own hands. She thought it would be a good idea to pump me full of laxative, something she would often take for herself.

Bending my naked body over in the bathroom, my bottom facing her, she would push two very large suppositories into my back massage, the pain was unreal, I remember crying saying please mum don't I will try and go to the toilet.

Mother had no patience for this or me. Medication is what she knew, so in her eyes she was doing the right thing. After about a month of this happening over and over I ended up in hospital, on the children's ward.

The doctors all scratching their heads, not knowing where my pain was coming from or why.

I never said anything to them and neither did mother. Several times I went in, in the end they said you have IBS, this carried on to my adulthood. Was it caused by the lack of knowledge back then? Was it caused by all the adult med's my mum gave me? I don't have the answer to this, who knows?

With the migraines, I could see lots of colours flashing past my eyes, the pain in my head I could not explain. Mother would lock me in the little room with the curtains shut, it was pitch black.

I remember banging my head on the door to let me out. I would bash my head, my forehead continually thinking it would take the pain away and wanting the door to open.

My head so bruised, mum would just cut another section of my fringe a little thicker to cover this, it was hidden well. The mouth ulcers I was made to swish my mouth out with salt water, you know when you have a tiny one and you get salt on it, it's very painful, imagine the extent of my mouth ulcers, I still remember nearly hitting the roof.

I could not eat, the only thing that helped for what was minutes would be a cup of tea or some ice cream.

The pain from all of these problems I was having was making me so frustrated, I only wanted to harm myself more. I only know now that my own mental health was suffering. No one cared, just an attention seeking child!!!

That's the thing, I was a child, living with a parent that could hardly cope with herself let alone me, her health was in bits, no one saw that I was suffering too.

It angers me today, that even now in my forties, I still suffer, I suffer with C.E.M Those that are not familiar with this, it's known as Childhood Emotional Maltreatment. A subject not talked about enough, even today.

It has huge effects on children, which takes you and follows you into your adult life. There is so much literature and research that shows the negative impact of C.E.M, but no research focuses on the devastating effects on the clinical side.

C.E.M is brought on by sexual, physical and mental abuse. It increases the risk of depression, anxiety, substance use and many more emotional problems.

C.E.M is taken to your adulthood, you find it hard to trust, value yourself, body image, relationships, eating disorders are all part of the battle. When you have C.E.M you have extremely low levels of self-worth, you don't cope with stress or self-criticism, you definitely find it hard to be loved.

Are you thinking ok, you live with a woman who is clearly suffering with her own health, and mental health, you suffer from mouth ulcers, headaches, bowel troubles, as well as insomnia and anaemia, does this really make you suffer with C.E.M.

I think it's a mixture of everything, what I have seen, heard and felt, no child should ever go through this at any age. All the symptoms of my health issues were my bodies way of saying I was not coping.

Time and time again I say this through my book of writing, that my siblings' story is their story, their memories are there to share with you only if one day they choose to write a book maybe, in the future, I know I would read it.

But being told you are the golden child, the un touched child, you always think of what they went through will never happen to me right? Because I am the privileged one hey!

COME ON!!! I had a TV yes, a sofa in my room, all I never asked for all put there off my dead Nan.

So surely I could never have any emotions or suffer right.? I am the lucky one after all. Well your wrong, so wrong. Let me tell you my first encounter of NOT being the golden child.

This I am afraid was done by the hands of my own mother, our mother whom I lived on my own with.

I had not long come out of hospital, suffering again from sleep deprivation, which would cause me to have night terrors. These were not your ordinary nightmares. This was when you could not wake up from a terror that was occurring, sometimes you thought you had woke up, to then quickly realise you had not. Brought on by stress.

This one night I was absolutely terrified, I ran into my mum's room, I woke her up, which believe me took some effort, after her sleeping pills. I was crying I just wanted some reassurance, some comfort, some love, someone to just tell me everything is going to be ok.

My mother held me tight in her arms and brought me close to her chest, for a split second I felt safe and secure and even loved.

My mother was holding me very tightly by now, her grip was getting tighter I could feel myself getting hotter and uncomfortable, I did not want to go back into my bedroom I was far too scared so I said nothing.

My eyes were open looking at my mum's face, mum's eyes were shut she was breathing heavy still holding tight.

She began to press her chest her breasts against me, over and over, at first I thought she was dreaming, but unfortunately she was awake, her legs then wrapped around my little body, my little frail thin body that was now very sweaty.

She pressed against me over and over sliding up and down, groaning, louder and louder, I knew this was not right, I tried to shout out, my mouth open but no words would come out, so I just kept still, so still, until I passed out and the sexual act was over.

My nighty was all wet, her grip had loosened as she had fell back to sleep, I wriggled out from her arms and crept quietly back into my room, my dark scary room, where I stood naked holding my wet nighty, wondering what the hell had just happened to me, and why.

I got a dry nighty out of my drawer, popped it on my cold wet body and lay on my bed, waiting for daylight to appear. I was not crying, I was numb, what will the morning bring?

Will my mum remember what she had done to her child? A child that just wanted some comfort, some love, but instead this child, me, got basically dry humped by her mother, for want of a better word.

My mum had just sexually abused me, how could I face her? how would she face me? would I tell anyone? Would they believe me? All alone once again with just my thoughts.

The golden Child....
The untouched Child...
The Privileged one.........

Chapter 7 - Keeping Mum Happy

Daylight appeared, I must have fallen to sleep, my eyes were all crusty in the corners, I must have been crying while asleep. Still lying in my bed, I gaze up to the ceiling, and remember what happened last night. I turn over and bring my legs to my chest and hold onto my knees, putting the covers over my head.

How will I go downstairs, face my mum? Will she say anything to me, will I say anything to her? For now, I was confused, numb, upset, and scared of the outcome.

I sat up, wiped my eyes, put my tiny thin feet onto the threadbare carpet wiggling my toes, looking around the room, seeing my dirty nightie on the floor. I reach for my dressing gown popping each of my thin arms into the gown, sitting back down and holding myself, while I wonder what I was going to do.

I picked myself up and went over to the curtains, opening them slowly, the sun shone through, it was so bright it hurt my eyes, my swollen red eyes. I quickly closed the curtains again, sat back down on the edge of the bed, my head spinning with my thoughts.

Come on Katherine get up and go down stairs, I had to face it at some point. Walking over to my shut door, my hand on the round handle, I slowly turn it, the handle squeaked, as did the floor boards, nothing in this house was quiet, everything made noises.

Walking on my tip toes, to the landing, I glance at Mum's room, her door wide open and her bed all made, she was down stairs. Off I go to my peep hole on the landing to see if I could see her or hear her. I could not see her, the chair where she usually sat, rolling her smokes and drinking tea was empty.

I could not hear her, where was she? Everywhere seemed so still and quiet. Big deep breath Katherine, as I take myself down the stairs.

The kitchen door was closed tightly, it was never closed that tight, only at night time, to keep the dog in. Nervously I opened the door fully, and there on the cold tiled floor was my mum, just lying there so still.

My approach had frozen, I could not go any further, all I did was stand very still with my feet switching on the cold floor, staring at my mum lying there.

I walked over, step by step, just staring, why was I not screaming, crying? This I do not know, I got to my mum's lifeless body, I could see her arms all bleeding, she had passed out too.

The usual thing for me to do would be to run to my Auntie Pam's 5 doors down or ring the number of the hospital on top of the phone. I had done this many times. Why was this time different? I stood over her just looking.

The times it had happened before, walking into the bathroom seeing your mum, lying in cold bath water with her arms hanging over the side of the bath, you watch the blood drip from her wrists onto the bath mat.

Running down the stairs to call for help, while you watch everyone around you rushing in and the ambulance guys and social workers. Off she goes to hospital again!

When you see her on the kitchen floor, back against the cupboard, holding a pair of scissors in her chest, that she had stabbed herself with. Off to hospital she goes again.

When you walk into the living room, to see the bottle of pills, on the floor, your mother frothing at the mouth. Off to hospital she goes again.

When you walk in from school to see your mum, hanging from the banister of upstairs, not enough to kill herself, but enough. Off to hospital she goes again.

Why was today different from any of the other times? Why was I not ringing Auntie Pam, the ambulance?

Today I stood over my mother's body, my long brown hair hanging over my face, as I watch my mum's arms bleed from the razor she had used this time, looking at her weak body just so still on the floor.

All I could think of was what had happened to me last night. Had my mother self-harmed once again, to punish herself, because she knew it was wrong, to take advantage of her child in this way?

I gasped at my thoughts, turning to the telephone, I walked over, picked the large receiver up and started to dial the number, glancing back to my mother on the floor. The number I had dialled so many times before. Off to hospital she goes again!

I never did tell anyone of that night, not until today, today when I put pen to paper and write this book.

My mum lived after yet another stomach pump, her wounds were healing, more scars to add to the many she already had. She would often say how she felt her skin crawling, like there was something inside her, she only knew to cut her skin to stop the feeling.

I was the child in our relationship, but I never felt I could be, why did I not tell anyone? The answer, I do not know!

I chose my mum, I chose to have a mum no matter what. All I ever wanted was for mum to be looked after and loved, so if that meant keeping this a secret for 40 years then so be it.

Every time she came out of hospital I would think this time it will be different, she will not do it again, things never changed, I changed, I learnt how to keep mum happy.

That's what I did kept mum happy, hoping that one day life would be oh so different.

I wanted to be the perfect daughter, to hope that one day I would have that perfect mum. Mum loved it when we made her happy, it was nice to see her smile, her happiness brought us happiness, it was just easier this way.

Setting ourselves little games to play, buying each other little gifts, no more than 1 pound, she found this fun, she was in a good place, we needed to keep it that way.

Then this one day, mum said, "*If you want anything you can just take it you know* "

What did this even mean?

I became a very fast learner. We went to the shops, supermarkets, I would watch my mum, just casually pop things into her basket, one for the basket one for the bag, yes, her bag!

Maybe down her pants, whatever she could do to hide, but we never paid for any of it. Mum would be so happy when we got home, with all her new items, food, clothes, make up.

She taught me well and sure enough before I knew it, I was very good at it indeed.
Nothing to be proud of at all, but it was just another normal thing we did, or so I thought.
A game of survival.

The only one time we got caught what I can remember of it was, going to the police station, watching the man in the uniform grab my mums' hand and roll my mum's finger tips in black ink, holding her fingers tight as he pressed each one onto the paper into the square boxes.

She still got away lightly with this though. She was quite a good actress when she needed to be, the water works would flood out, then the mental health nurse would come, a quick slap on the wrist and back home we were.

My mum would be laughing at this point, she did not care, she now had a criminal record.

Not only did my talented mother teach me how to paint, draw, sew, she now added stealing to the list of things.

Survive and lie she would say, it's the only way in this world, this is how her mind worked. I still did it though, it made her happy to get new things.

Mother had ditched men, for the first time in a very long time, we were not living with a man in the house. Nope she had moved onto women, yep women.

At first it was the odd magazine I would find, magazine just with women in, in sexual context. Was this why my mum did those things to me? Because now she like girls, so confused, but as usual I just got on with it.

To be honest I preferred the girls in the house to the men, they did not make me feel uneasy, it was like having lots of mum's. We would play card games together, twister, we had some really fun times.

Mum was less stressed, the house was a happy house for the first time in a real long time or so I thought.

Before I knew it, mum was not with the ladies anymore, she was by herself again, this only meant she would lean on me more.

This one day she was screaming with her back, she really did suffer with her back, and discs, I think she slipped them a number of times. I ran upstairs to see what all the screaming was about.

Mum was on the bathroom floor, holding her stomach, I could see blood everywhere, I did not know where it was coming from. She shouted clean it up, clean it up! So I did, I got toilet paper and started to clean the blood away, flushing the paper down the toilet, feeling sick in my mouth and still not knowing where this blood was coming from.

She opened her legs, still screaming in pain, the blood was all over her underwear, she made me take them off, clean her up, and then asked me to insert a tampax.

I was off the age where I did not know why she was bleeding from her private area, I looked at the long cotton wool like stick thing with string hanging from it, she guided me to where it needed to go, while staring at me in the eyes.

I hated every moment of it, I quickly washed my hands and helped mum onto the bed. I thought ok, this is me helping her, it became a regular occurrence, just sometimes there was never any blood.
We kept mum HAPPY!

I did not want her to go back to hospital, so I did everything I needed to do.

Why I hear you ask, well I was older now and my dad had stopped taking me to grandma's. I was allowed to stay home alone now, I did not want that, so I helped and kept mum happy the only way I knew how to.

Dad had got married and had another child, his new wife did not like the fact that her husband, my dad had another child, so we became distant.

For some time, my dad had found happiness, got a new family, I was not to be part of that. I think my mum was secretly pleased I saw less and less of him.

I would call him Father Christmas because the only time I would see him would be this time, it broke my heart to know I had a brother, I would not grow up with.

It broke me to know that this little boy would get the family of mum and dad, they would have all the special times, the Christmas dinners together, Easter time, birthdays, while I was left just with my mum to cope, to pick up the pieces, while dealing with adolescence and trying to figure life out, and keeping my own mental health, as healthy as it could be.

Feeling very alone, the only person I had was my mum. Was this it for me? The broken little girl, caring for her parent, was this to be my life, forever and ever?

Then another man moved in, my mum seemed to like taxi men, yup it was another one. He seemed different, we would go on holiday together.

I would share a room with my mum and the new man, I would have to listen to them having sex, while I pretended to be asleep.

They would go off for the day together on holiday, leave me some lunch money and leave me around the pool by myself. Crazy when I think of this now, but at the same time, I grew to like my own company.

I found I could just go up to people and start talking to them, making friends easy, being the clown, making everyone happy, smiling and laughing while crying inside, this became normal life.

Back home the new man worked funny hours, mum liked him working, she loved having extra money and being treated to nice things.

I walked into the front room, the man was sitting on the sofa watching TV, he said "*come sit with me Katherine*".

I walked over very awkward and went to sit on the sofa next to him, he then pulled my arm really hard and sat me on his knee. He said "*put your arm around my neck Katherine your mum said it's ok to give me hugs*"

Part of me thought for that split second, he was trying to be a father figure trying to be nice to me. My arm went around his shoulder, he was a large man, with a pot belly, he smelt of sweat.

"*There you go Katherine that feels nice doesn't it?*" No!! It did not, I felt uncomfortable sat there on his knee in my little skirt and top, with my white knee high socks.

He reached for my other hand and started to force my hand into his trousers. I could feel the hardness of his penis, he started to thrust me on his knee while forcing my hand, I did not scream, I did not shout, I just sat there helpless, not wanting my mum to come in, she was only in the kitchen.

I thought Katherine just go with it, mum seems so happy with this man she will never believe me if I told her, it was best to keep this to myself.

I then heard my mum walking through the hallway, the man quickly stopped his actions, my mum entered the room, I was still sitting on his knee at this point, She shouted "*Katherine get off at once your far too old to sit on people's knees*". So, I jumped off, shaking inside and ran to my room.

The look in my mum's eyes she knew, she knew what he was doing, but men before kids remember.

Chapter 8 - Treatment

Life just got a whole lot more complicated. We were now living with a man that makes my mum extremely happy, but a man that had eyes, for her little girl. Were all men like this?

Going to school to see my friends and of course Craig, gave me normality, it gave me hope, that life would and could be different. Looking at my friends' parents, looking at Craig's parents, seeing that you can make a good life for yourself, you can be loved in the right way. I knew then I had to get my head down at school, work hard, save money, and get out!

I had just got in from school, my mum was nowhere to be found. My Auntie Pam was there, "*your mum has gone into hospital again Katherine*" my answer, "*what has she done this time?*".

"*Nothing*" was the reply, "*she has gone to get the help she needs Katherine, she's gone to get better once and for all*".

I did not understand, what I did understand is that she was not sick with a bug, she had something so severe, who and what was going to get her better? I thought we just had to live with this forever and a day.

"She is having electric treatment."
Can you imagine telling a child that her mother is going to have electric treatment, what the hell did that even mean?

My first thoughts were, her in a chair, like what you see on horror films being tortured. The thing was my mum was a tortured soul, a soul so lost, I honestly believe she knew what the new man was doing and she wanted to get help, I took some comfort from this.

Time had moved on, research into new medications and treatments for Mental Health were coming, but electric treatment sounded like the dark ages to me, it was basically a helmet onto your head where they send electric currents to balance the chemical that was not inline.

Sounds spooky right? Nope this is normal guys, why was I not shocked? I think that may have not been the right word to write...ha.

My Auntie Pam took care of me for the duration of time my mum was having treatment. I would lie awake in bed wondering if this really would cure my mum, would I have a real mum?

Someone that is completely better, would she look different, sound different? all these wonderful thoughts going over in my mind.

The day came, my mum was coming home after her treatment. For the first time in a long time I was excited but nervous, as this meant me going back home with the new man in the house.

There were yet more surprises and changes, the new man was not there anymore, had he got fed up waiting for my mum to return? Oh no, his wife had found out, yes you heard right, the new man had a wife and six children.

He had been living a double life, I always thought he worked odd hours. How can anyone lead two different lives is beyond me? We went on holiday, he lived with us, and also did the same with his wife and children, how bloody strange.

But relief had set in, it was back to just me and mum again now, even though that was hard, I could cope more with just my mum. In my mind though I could only think of his children, and was he like that with them? I would never know, I never did speak up, it haunts my soul.

Mum was awfully tired on her return and slept loads. We had new people coming in to check on her, as well as her long-suffering friend Auntie Pam.

Mum seemed different, was I just hoping or was she actually different? I watched her walk into the little room, she walked up to the Doll's, touched their faces, ran her hand down their sock like bodies, and quickly turned to me and said, *"What the hell are these"*?

"Mum you made them, you made us a family of Doll's" She looked horrified, she walked past me quickly and went under the sink, that is where we kept all the stuff like bleach and bin bags etc. She got the roll of bin bags and started to wrap each doll up, laying them onto the floor, and making sure everything was covered.

There it was, the Dolls were in bin bag's, three life like bodies lying on the floor, it looked awful if anyone was to come in, it looked like my mum had just murdered three people and was getting rid of the bodies, I stood and watched quietly as always.

One at a time she carried them upstairs, placing them on the floor of the landing, she then went back downstairs to fetch a chair, quickly carrying it up the stairs, I just looked on thinking her back seems ok now, but I said nothing.

She climbed onto the chair, then put her feet on to the back of the chair balancing, looking up to the hatch, the loft hatch, she shouted me to help. I passed each doll to her as she placed them on to the floor of the attic, that was it, three dolls' in bin bags in the attic. The hatch got closed, the chair taken down stairs.

My mum sat back on the chair, lit a fag, popped the kettle on, looked over to me and smiled. Like a true smile, I felt good about it, she was different, her medication was different, she was more mellow, we never spoke about the doll's again.

My mum had lost parts of her memory due to the treatment. What parts had she lost? Well making the dolls for one! Did she still remember all the bad stuff?

At this point in my life, for the first time ever, I did not care, I got glimpses of a Mother. A mother I always wanted, she started to bake again, we had home cooked meals, my clothes and bedding were washed, she was happy, and I was happy. How could this treatment of worked, who knows? I had a mum, I knew she was in there somewhere, it just took this to make it happen.

Obviously, I had not lost my memory, and still would cry at night, still had night terror's, still not going in to mum's room just in case, still writing my notes and popping them under the floorboards, but I noticed a change in my words.

I noticed a change in me. I was gaining a little weight, the mouth ulcers were not as bad, I had not had a headache, and no hospital visits about my bowels and stomach, the anxiety was leaving my body for the time being.

Yes, I would never forget what I had seen, heard or felt, but I wanted a mum, a mum in any shape, size or form. Just a mum to be the same as everyone else, to fit in.

I started to move on, I embraced this woman that stood there before me, she was trying so hard. I even started to tell her I loved her and she would say it back, we would hug and it was ok.

Mum had re decorated throughout, goodbye to the murals, she even had a job. We had no men in the house, just me, mum and the dog, things were looking up.

I started to help my mum instead of pushing her away. I feel I was understanding her condition more, hard to believe I know, but so is Mental Health and to keep my Mental Health and Mum's Mental Health going ok I became the daughter she should have had.

Going to school got easier knowing I was coming home to a meal for the very first time. I knew I would not find my mum passed out on the floor, she stopped self-harming.

Her passion as always became her garden, she completely changed it, it was a work of art, it looked amazing. The house was starting to look like a normal house too since getting her job cleaning.

She was able to get a catalogue so was ordering lots of new furniture, she still painted everywhere herself, but it was more neutral.

We now had a peachy cream front room with new carpet and sofa. I know all this seems so small, but this progress was massive, and it made such a difference into our lives.

So much so, I felt it was time to let Craig know where I really lived, yup, that's how massive of a change this was.

I came home from school, sat at the table as I always did while mum dished my tea out. She never did eat with me, she would have a cup of tea and a fag and watch me eat.

Of course, I would eat it all, in school I was only eating rubbish, so it was good to have a warm home cooked meal. My mum's food tasted so good, her cooking had gone amazing, or was it just me being so grateful for change that everything seemed good?

I plucked up the courage to tell her about Craig, I felt I could talk to her, I did not feel so alone anymore. I went on to say about a boy I had met, and I had feelings for him and was he allowed to come around to our house, yes!!!

I wanted Craig to come around, to meet my mum, I just had to figure out how I was going to tell him about where I really lived, or do I just say we moved?

Ha no, enough was enough of lying, secrets, the darkness was lifting from home life, things were ok, so it was time for me to find my inner strength and just go for it, would mum say yes? Would Craig be angry I had Lied? Could I finally have someone to hear my words?

My mum smiled when I told her, asking me lots of questions, I even told her I had lied about where we lived.

"*Were you ashamed of me Katherine*?" she said. "*No not at all Mum, I just knew you would not like me having a boyfriend or bringing anyone around*"

Here I go again lying, but I could not say yes, I was ashamed of you, could I? I could not say everyone thinks you're crazy mum, I could not say about any of the past. She was in a good place, a really good place, so I thought a little white lie would not hurt anyone.

I did not want my mum to go backwards, I did not want things to change, so I kept my true thoughts to myself. Always knowing what made mum happy so I carried on.

She seemed excited to hear of Craig, she said to me "*Does he smoke? Does he drink? Is he good to you?*"

"Mum he's like 15, of course he does not smoke or drink and yes he is good to me"
And then I thought of course she is going to ask me all this. She had her first child when she was 15, she had three children by 19.

Yes, I understood, she was making sure, she was looking out for me, she was caring, she was being a MUM!!!

Just I was not use to this, so it took some time to adjust to the new woman I called mum.

I will be honest, parts of me wondered did she really lose her memory, or was that an easier way of her coping? I often thought how can someone change like this so fast?

Was there going to be dark times again? was there going to be hospital visits? was there going to be any more men? all of these things I felt.

I said nothing though, I just focused on the positive things, like Craig, my friends, my siblings, and now my mum.

It's at this same time I start to see my dad a little again. He had bought a video shop next to the hair salon it was easier for me to go there to see him, as I was not welcome at his home.

I would call and see him in the evenings, we would chat about life and even talk about mum and how well she was doing. I had missed him, I always Loved my dad even though he was not the dad dreams are made of, but I think it's obvious by now I was far from living the fairy-tale lifestyle.

I just thought to myself how lucky I am to have a mum and dad, not perfect at all but they are mine, some kids out there don't get this privilege at all, so I took what I had and went with it.

I would help my dad out at the video shop, and he would pay me a little pocket money, I did not say anything to mum another white lie just to keep things sweet.

I look back and think I should have been worrying about puberty and growing up, but instead I had a whole host of troubles I carried with me.

It was ok, I started to grow up, started to build my wall of strength, my thick layer of skin, wearing a mask as I always did. I just got on with it, there were plenty worse off than me, right?

I had my dad back in my life, I had my mum, I had a boyfriend, all I needed was love.

I could not exist in a life without love, it had taken me to this stage in my life to realise this, I craved love, the thing was, would I allow myself to be loved?

Chapter 9 - Strength

For the first time, I felt focused on me, sounds selfish, but for most of my childhood the focus was on mum. I am still a child at this point. I focused on school, got my head down, did my work. I was good at it, getting top marks in all aspects of lessons, one main one being drama studies, with a lovely teacher Miss Porter.

She just got me, I do not know how much the school knew about home life, but she seemed to have so much time for me. She knew I had a talent, she had compassion, she was the best teacher ever. She had long dark hair to her waist, she was extremely small in height, always in joggers and tiny pumps, her feet were so small, no makeup at all, just naturally beautiful.

I felt myself building a trust, a bond, when I look back, trusting people was a huge thing, it still is, but she was different, her heart was good I could feel it.

I would stay after school for extra drama lessons. I felt I could lose myself, be someone I was not, I loved becoming different characters and using different voices, I had humour it came so naturally, at last something I had found.

So that was it, I wanted to be an actress, I wanted to make it big, I wanted it to work out so much. I would think, if I can do this then I could raise enough money to get my own place. I could definitely do this, I was determined.

So I set myself tasks, really stepping out of my comfort zone, not worrying what friends thought, I just knew I had to do it, I could see the end goal, I wanted it so so much.

Now mum was what I thought better, we both got a job at the local farm. This was a farm open to the public where you can pet the animals and have horse riding lessons, a farm park.

We used to walk there, it was about 3 miles away but that's what you did back then. My mum never did drive because of her meds making her sleepy, so we walked. If we had spare money which was rare, we would get the bus home. Mum worked in the cafe, I would look after the horses. Instead of payment I got to ride at the end of the day, this became another passion.

I would feel free on the back of the horse, just me in charge of such a beast, such a spiritual animal. The horse would listen as I spoke softly to him, no saddle no reins, just me bareback holding onto the mane, cantering through the fields.

I felt alive, free and that I could achieve absolutely anything. My Mum also enjoyed the cafe, she was meeting new people and building her confidence.

She would get cash in hand but it made her happy and for the first time ever it was something we did together, mother and daughter time, I loved it.

I would go there every Sunday. Once home I said to my mum I wanted to get a job on a Saturday too, not at the farm, but in our local city of Chester.

I wanted to earn some money, I was getting a little pocket money off my dad from the video shop, but I was striving for more.

It was then it really did hit home, how determined I was to become, how focused on what I wanted, setting goals huge goals at such a young age, I had a plan.

I did not want to share my plans with my mother, I did not want her to know I was planning to save and move out, follow my dreams of becoming an actress. I did not want to spoil her mood, her happiness she had found, her peace even. So, I kept it to myself.

I got the train to Chester. Craig would walk me through the town to the station, he was just finishing his paper round on his BMX bike. He would wheel the bike and pop his arm around me and wished me luck on the search of work, a Saturday job in the city.

The train arrived we kissed, god I liked his lips so much touching mine it felt so right. Craig did not know of my plans, I was keeping this close to my chest, I was only a teenager, I did not want to scare him.

The train arrived at Chester station having no idea where I am going I head into town where all the shops are. I went into the first shop up to the counter where the woman was already judging me I could tell.

I was wearing jeans and a shirt and of course my red lippy. My hair was long and curly now, it was massive, I would tip my head upside down, to make it even bigger, I loved it. Nervously I ask "*Is there any Saturday jobs going?*"

The answer was no, huge sigh, but I had took the biggest plunge by walking in there, so on to the next.

I arrived at a very tall glass building three storeys high, it was huge. Large glass doors, where two men like security guards were leaning on the door. The men were Indian, wearing Indian clothes, all the clothes on display in the window were very out there.

But as you know my mother made my clothes, so I thought why not, let's go and ask in here. Passing the two tall men on the doors, they smiled and said hello, it seemed ok. OMG!!

This shop was massive, filled with rail after rail of clothes, hundreds of styles. The counter was big, five tills, all with girls behind them, they were not Indian.

Slowly walking up trying to find my inner confidence that drama lessons had taught me, I coughed for attention and politely asked for a Job, to my surprise the lady said yes come in next Saturday and we will get you trained and started, it will be in the stock room upstairs.

Stock room! I did not care where the bloody hell it was, oh my days Katherine you just gone and got a job. I had got my very first paid Job of twelve pounds working at 8am to 6pm, on Saturdays.

Child labour I know but it was money and it was thirty years ago, so twelve pounds was a huge amount.

When I got home I was so excited to tell my mum, I could hardly get my words out. Her first words were not congratulations I am so proud of you, her first words were how much are you getting?

I stood and stared at her big brown eyes, I felt like I was so excited, but my mum was not, I do not know why but I said ten pounds, instead of twelve pounds. My mum's reply was "*Good, good, you can give me five pounds of that towards the telephone bill and washing your clothes.*"

Five pounds I screamed inside, it would hardly be worth me going, working 10 hours to pay my mum too. My heart sank, all my enjoyment of the day just left my body, I got a glimpse of the old mum back, I said nothing.

I was still in school, why did I have to give my mum money? I just did not get it at all, but so pleased I said ten pounds instead of twelve, I had to pay my train fare out of it too, what a bloody nightmare.

But I was set on my plan, my goal, so I did go to work every Saturday, for ten hours. I got a dinner break and two 15-minute breaks too.

I met loads of new friends, one was older than me and she was lovely. She started to pick me up to go to work in her car, so that saved me some money. I would have seven pounds to myself, give my mum five, I would save the rest.

Some of the girls I worked with would spend their wages on clothes at the end of the day. They would ask if I was going to do the same, I did not, I was saving for my future, it may only of been seven pounds a week, twenty eight pounds a month, but for me, it was massive.

Hiding the money each week in my bedroom under the carpet where the floorboards were loose, where I used to write my notes. Now I was saving notes, back then we had one-pound notes, so you can imagine how many I had ha ha ha.

I started to go to the local youth club with my friends, Craig would be there playing pool any excuse to see him.

My clothes were still either charity or handmade, some now and then for birthdays I would get a new coat or PJ's. My friends all growing up and they too also had weekend jobs, their clothes were so nice compared to mine, I did feel left out, and I do regret what I did next.

Reading backwards you can remember what my mum taught me growing up, even though we no longer did this together, I was not sure if mum did. I still remembered what to do.

I would ask to go on the changing rooms shift, and when no one was looking, I would grab an outfit, pop it on then put my own clothes over the top, yep you guessed it I got into the habit of getting myself a new outfit every week.

The two Indian guys on the door were security and they would check your bag as you left but they never did check you. I do not think they would be allowed to body search and lucky for me I just walked out like the world owed me something. I was so happy to have all these new clothes, no one in work ever did notice, the shop was huge.

At the time I had no guilt, only now as an adult I do.

My mum saw all the new clothes and just thought I was spending my wages, well what I had left, but nope, I was stealing them and still saving my seven pounds a week under the floor.

They made me feel good, feel more confident, for the first time ever I was fitting in. Craig would compliment me on my outfits, and my friends would say wow where did you get that from, so in a way I was sending people to spend money in the shop. I was just advertising their clothes that is what I told myself anyhow.

I was becoming entrepreneurial I did not even know it, just a slight hiccup on breaking the law, but when you have been taught by your own mother, what could possibly go wrong? and I did look good.

Back to school in my new shiny green bomber jacket, I had never been so trendy. Miss Porter came running over to me *"Katherine I have wonderful news"* Oh my gosh what could it be I thought.

She grabbed both of my little hands and held them tight, *"Katherine I have got you an audition"*
Audition I thought, audition for what?

Well it happened to be a new series on ITV called Children's ward, it was a hospital drama, she went on to say, you fit the bill, the criteria is just you, this is your chance Katherine your chance to shine!

Excitement, oh my lord I could not contain my excitement, but me being me I found it very hard to show it externally, but inside I was buzzing, what do I have to do?

You have to go along to an audition with lots of other children who want the part, "*I believe in you Katherine you can so do this.*" So, most kids would run home to their parents screaming their news from the rooftops, but not me, I went home that day and said nothing.

I just did not know how to say it, how she would react, would she then know I wanted to leave home? It's just me and her, she would not cope on her own without me I thought.

I had to find my inner strength to speak up, I could not go to Manchester Auditions on my own, I would need a parent Miss Porter explained. I was hoping she could of come with me but it had to be your guardian. Katherine, I shouted at myself, just tell her, tell my own mum for god sake, what is the worst that could happen?

That was It! I knew what could happen and It scared me. So, I told my dad instead. I thought we could go in secret.

I thought he would be proud and as excited as me, this was my chance. "*Katherine I cannot take time off work to take you to an audition, do not build your hopes on this Katherine.*"

That plan did not go to plan, I had no choice, I had to tell my mother about everything. About my dreams, hopes, aspirations, what I wanted for a future. I could only hope she was in a good place of understanding, a place where she too would be proud, for her to see I wanted a future, a life very different to what it was now.

Would she understand? would all my dreams come true? I had to tell her, I found the strength, the courage and told her everything.

Chapter 10 - Letting Go!

"*What do you mean you have an audition?*"
My mother's reply, to what I had just told
her. I explained everything, so Katherine do
you think you can make money from this?

Money was on my mind because I knew I
needed it to get a life of my own, but at the
same time, my mum also loved money,
other people's that is. I just replied with "*I
have not thought of that!*"

Just another little white lie, Truth was I did
not know what money would be involved it
had not been discussed, but I just wanted to
go along to the audition.

My Mother knew Manchester well, so she
agreed. I could not believe it. That morning
the morning of the audition, I made sure I
had rolled enough roley's for my mum, her
cup of tea was made, her medication, laid
out on the kitchen top, I wanted nothing to
upset the day.

I was not worrying about the audition, I was worrying to make sure my mum stayed on track and her anxiety did not kick in. Miss Porter was meeting us there.

Lots and lots of other kids were all lining up to take the audition, we just went into a room, where there was a table with three people sat behind. We were given a piece of paper with our lines on, Miss Porter had taught me too well how to improvise.

So I had no nerves, only the nerves I carried for my mum. I knew she would be on her own, well with Miss Porter, I hoped she was not rude. To be fair, my mum was pretty good with strangers now.

I walked into the room, it's my turn. I turned my head to look at my mum for reassurance, but she was busy chatting to a man, a dad of another child, it did not take her long at all to chat to men ha!

The door closed, I did my stuff and left, it was over in what felt like seconds. "*What now my mum said?*" Miss porter quickly replied, "*we have to wait now, we go home and if Katherine is successful then we will receive a phone call at the school*", they had Miss Porter's home number too.

I sighed a big sigh it was over, just a waiting game now, that's all we could do. We all got the train home. I was really proud of my mum for taking me, for being there, for being mum.

She went on to say how she loved watching Coronation Street, and hoped that one day I was in that, and she would be proud of me, we laughed at this thought.

Later that evening my mum said would you like to go to Granada Studio's? I could not believe what I was hearing, yes, yes please mum I shouted. She said we can go for a tour around where they film Coronation Street, see what it's like, I will have to save up, but you can take a friend too.

I could only think I was dreaming, but no, this was happening. I was going on a tour of the TV studio's; would I meet the cast I thought?

You never know they could be filming that day, so so excited. A Mum and daughter day, this is all I ever wanted and guess what it was happening. I invited my best friend Auntie Pam's Son, he was excited too.

The day came, we got the train again to Greater Manchester and we spent the whole day at the studio's. I felt so good, I had more new clothes on. Light blue denim Jeans, white T shirt and a floral print blazer.

My hair all done curly just like mum's, she even let me pop a reddish wash in wash out colour on, she had the same on her hair. She wore a dress she had made and her Mum's old cream mac, she even wore Heels. I looked at her and felt proud to call her Mum.

We had a really special day, looked around the cobble streets, the row of houses, cars and much more. I remember this day like no other, I was with my mum and my best friend, no man to worry about just us. Was life really turning around? I think it was doing mum good not having a man in her life, I know it was doing me the world of good.

After a really special day, we got home, the phone rang, it was Miss Porter. My heart was beating so fast I knew she was ringing for one thing only, to tell me the news of the audition. I held the heavy black receiver to my ear very tight, I listened, and then put the phone down without even saying anything.

My mum turned to me and said *"Do not worry Katherine there will be other times."*

Tears just dropped out of my eyes, I had no control of my feelings, *"Mum, I got it, I got the part!"* *"Oh my god Katherine that's wonderful news."*

I could not believe what was happening. I had my Mum trying so hard, I had a boyfriend, and now I had just got a part in a TV series. This was it I told myself, this was it, this is going to help me turn my life around, this is my chance I thought.

I could not wait to get to school and see Miss Porter, what were the next plans? when would this start? it was all I could think about. I do not remember even telling my dad! I was in a whirl, I did not want it to stop.

Miss Porter called me over, *"Katherine"* She said it so serious, I was worried, *"Do Not worry Katherine"*

Now I knew I needed to when someone tells you this, you know something is coming you might not want to hear.

Miss Porter went on, *"Katherine you now need an agent and an equity card, you can apply for these, but they will cost money will that be a problem?"*

Inside my head I shout....OF COURSE it will be a FUCKING PROBLEM!!! We do not have any money.

It was going to cost in the hundreds, to be represented and insured to fulfil the requirements at the time, I knew we did not have it, what could I do now?

I get home and tell my mum, I knew what she would say, I hated asking, I did not want to put pressure on her. I knew we did not have it, even the money I had saved from working was not going to cover this, I could only ask my dad, and that is what my mum said.

This too was a no, my dad said he did not have the money either to give me, he was still paying my mum money because I was in education, along with his two shops, and his house, he said he could not afford it either. What do I do???

I did what I could only do at 15, I let go of the dream, it broke my heart, all my dreams and hopes just came crashing down, when was my luck ever going to change.

I went into a dark time, a time I cannot explain. I just was not myself, whatever that was anyway. Just when I thought life was going to work out, I even let go of my job at the clothes shop in Chester, I just thought what is the point, what really is the point trying so hard? I nearly had it in my hands to only be taken from me once again due to the fact of money.

I started to play up at school, so out of character for me. I started to whack it, that is what we called it back then, I just did not go, well my mum thought I went but I did not.

I would stay at a friends who also whacked it from school. I did not like who I was becoming. I started to smoke, something I swore I would never do, I started to drink, go to pubs, night clubs, going out and staying out.

Craig was no longer around, not surprised really, I was turning into my mother, I had lost hope, everything I had been through, heard, felt, seen, I was so strong, but I had been strong for too long, I was slipping into depression, and I did not even know it.

I thought I was having a good time, acting hard, having different boys, what the hell was I thinking? I was throwing it all away, would I be queuing outside the chemist next for my latest fix?

On one night out I got beat up by five girls, I got myself home, god knows how, half my hair missing on one side, bruises on my face, legs and stomach. I just walked up stairs, sobbed myself to sleep, not even telling my mum.

I too was lost, the little girl, where had she gone? Trying to be an adult, but still only a child, with no guidance, no role model, but this was no excuse, the only one to fix this was me.

With all my self absorbedness of feeling sorry for myself, I had not even noticed my mum was sick again, she was lonely.

I was not there for her, too busy feeling the way I did, she was sleeping more, not going out, not washing, not doing much at all, before it got too bad, before she self harmed again, she admitted herself into hospital.

I was left home alone, been trying to act like an adult, but I was not. I was so lonely, just me and the dog, it gave me time to reflect on how I had been acting.

Enough was enough, time to get things back on track, pick myself up and start again. I promised myself I would not become the victim of my situation, I would become a survivor, (wise words from a true friend).

The one thing that was good in my life was Craig. Was it too late for us? Never really allowing him in completely and pushing him away when I needed him the most, the loneliness was unbearable.

I lay on my bed as I often did with just my thoughts running through my head, dosing in and out of sleep. I hear loud music playing, I thought I was dreaming, East 17, "*Stay Another Day*" still lying on my bed wondering where it was coming from, I sat up and walked over to my window. Lent on my black window sill, I pressed my forehead against the glass, there in the distance on the field, I could see Craig.

Craig was playing our song as loud as he could from his stereo, to get my attention. This boy I thought, this boy has been sent to me, it's time now to get that boy back. With him being there I knew he wanted me too. Finally sinking in how much he meant to me, finally allowing myself to feel what true love was.

Yes, we were young, our relationship built on a lot of likes on my behalf, at first, but now I have given my head the wobble it needed. "*Katherine go get your Boy*" I said to myself. Picking my little Jack Russell up in my arms and kissing her with Joy, she was my best friend, I popped her lead on, and ran with her to the field to meet Craig.

Tears are now rolling down my face, my nose running, but I did not care, I threw my arms around his neck, kissing him, like we had never kissed before, this was it for me, this was the boy I would spend the rest of my life with. He came back for me, even after what a mess I was, even knowing my background, he wanted me, and I wanted him.

Before I knew it, we were back at number 55. My mum still in hospital so we had the house to ourselves, holding each other so close, no words needed the energy we felt is all that mattered.

The little girl that thought she would never feel or want to feel love, just did, it felt right, real and exciting, my childhood love.

My mum was back from hospital, but she was not on her own, there was another man with her another man she had met on the ward, what was his story?

I did not have the energy for this, I was older now, back focused on what I wanted, I had love in my life, and all I wanted was for my mum to have that too, to be truly happy, would this be the man that did this?

I had taken myself back to school to finish my GCSE's, surprised myself with the results I had got, A* in drama, B in English and Media studies, C in Maths and a D in science, not bad for a girl with all that on her shoulders, proof you can put your mind to anything.

What will I do now? Pursue an acting career? Nope I went and got a hairdressing apprenticeship with my friend from school.

I got a job in a salon in Flint, it was not far from where I lived at 55, so I was able to get the bus. College supplied a coach for my one-day release to LLandrillo College, my two-year course to become a stylist, something I never really wanted to do, but it was a job, a paid job, £50 a week for 50 hours.

Why was I not going to work in my Dad's salon? I never did get asked, I knew I had to stand on my own two feet, with no help from no one.

The world did not owe me anything, still trying to fix myself, and work on myself every day, to be positive. What helped me the most was Craig and his family, being surrounded by normality was good for me. They were becoming my family too, accepting me, knowing how much we loved each other.

Craig had got an apprenticeship too. A Joinery one, earning himself £50 a week too. We both got on with it, working 5 days a week till late, seeing each other every night and every weekend. I loved it, took my mind off everything, building new friendships, while learning a skill, a skill that could get me my own place, I still craved this, I needed out of 55.

Mum was ok, the man she was with was diagnosed with severe mental health, she was caring for him, and she seemed to be happy doing so. He was kind and never did me any harm. He did not know of my mother in her younger days, only the woman she was now, I think this was best.

I finally felt, this was the right time for me to go, to go into the big bad world and fend for myself. I took it upon myself to go searching for flats to rent, truth was we just could not afford it right now. Time to work harder finish our apprenticeships and see what the future would hold for Katherine and Craig.

Chapter 11 - Moving Out.

We had now saved enough money to go on our very first holiday, a 2-week package holiday to the island of Ibiza. I was so chuffed to be able to do this with the boy who I now truly knew I loved.

He loved me too, we could not get enough of each other, this is just what we both needed, our first time of spending two solid weeks together in the sun, no stress, no work just us.

Once we arrived back off our holiday all tanned, Craig with his Spanish blood and his long hair looked like he could actually be full Spanish.

A very attractive boy, I keep saying boy, but we were growing up he was becoming a man, a man I wanted to grow old with. How could I know this just at the age of 17? I do not know, but I could not imagine life without him ever, and so good to know that he felt exactly the same, enough to ask me to get in engaged.

Yes, Craig had just asked me to get engaged, I could not be happier, of course I said yes. Just the small matter of telling his parents now, and of course mine.

My mum seemed happy for us, she was very wrapped up in her own life and relationship with this new man, to notice much.

I was out working all the time and my spare time was with Craig, so you could say we were drifting, more apart than we were before. Even though I always had my guard up, I was happy, my life was moving forward, and I had to focus on that.

I kept myself busy with work, in fact I found myself wanting to be busy all the time. I did not want to stop and have time to think about the earlier days, some would say a little manic myself, but if this is what I had to do to keep sane or, so I thought then so be it.

Craig's Parents seemed ok with it, not that happy just ok. I think they were worried we were young, they knew some of my back ground. It was their son and he was their priority, not that I felt this at the time, ha ha.

We saved some more money up, to have an engagement party, at our local Labour Club. Things like this just did not happen, I never had birthday parties, Christmas parties, so for me to be able to do this for us out of my own hard earnings then I was so so proud of myself, proud of us.

I knew in my heart of hearts that this was it for me, this would be the one and only time I would do this. I swore to myself I would not let the cycle happen to me, I would have one true love, just one.

I would work hard to make it work, to keep making it work, we were so open and honest with each other about this. Craig knew I had been bridesmaid so many times, for cousins, my dad, and my mum, so many weddings. It was set in my mind I would do this once. At the age of 17 still with my boyish frame, long brown hair, and crooked teeth, I just knew, I just knew.

Our Evening was everything I wanted it to be and more. Craig had bought me a ring, it was £40 from Argos, real gold with one stone. I could not believe it, what a lucky girl I was, how things were changing. I was making that happen, we were making that happen together.

Craig's mum, offered to do the food and pay for the cake, this was such a big help, we had a disco too, it was a proper grown up party just for us to celebrate our love together, our future.

I remember standing in the middle of the dance floor looking around, there was all Craig's family, brothers, aunties, uncles, cousins, nans and granddads, all of them. My friends all around, new friends and school friends, all coming together to celebrate with us.

What meant the most was, I looked over and there was my mum, just glowing, her face so so pretty with all her makeup on, of course I was wearing mine too, along with my red lipstick.

Mum had gone blonde now, still lots of curls, a little more weight. There she sat laughing and joking with my sister and her husband, their children were there, my niece and nephew, and two seats down was my dad with my younger brother.

Did I ever, ever imagine that this would happen? Nope not in a million years, but they did it for me, for Craig and I, in the same room, being ok with each other. When I think back of their past this was a massive step a huge positive massive step.

I glanced over at my love, my fiancé, took a deep breath in and skipped over to him wrapped my arms around him and said thank you.

He said "*why are you thanking me*?", "*Craig I just am*", and with that he laughed spun me around and we danced the night away to our favourite tunes, it was nothing but perfect.

After such a good weekend, back to work we went. It just made me want to live with Craig even more now.

We both worked so hard for our qualifications, and we both hit 18 and both qualified, me as a hairdresser and Craig a Joiner. This meant a pay rise from £50 to £70, not huge but enough, enough to be able to move out.

Of course, mum found out about the pay rise and took more money off me, so it made me even more determined to get a place, but everything we looked at we just could not afford.

Back in the salon, doing a lady's hair and we are chatting as you do when you're a stylist, you kind of find out more about them.

People found it very easy to open up to me, and I was a good listener, something from my childhood where I would just take it all in and just listen.

Any way we were chatting, and she mentioned she had a house, in fact she had a lot of houses that she rented out.

She went onto say she had one just come up was I interested? I looked at her in the mirror of the salon as I continued to blow dry her ever so thick hair, I remember it so well as it took me ages, which was good because I wanted to find out more.

I thought to myself I would never be able to afford a house, we had been looking at two bed flats and they were out of our price range once you consider bills etc. and that fact you have to eat too.

It was in Bagillt, not a place I was familiar with, but it was only 7 miles away a little village. She went onto to say it was a two up two down, what an earth was this I thought.

I nodded, and said sounds fantastic, but not sure I will be able to afford it. The lady, went on, "*If you look after it, decorate it etc. you can have it for £35 a week rent, the gas and electric are on a meter, and you have to sort your own water and rates out.*"

I switched the hairdryer off, held it in my hand still and just stared at her through the mirror, "*You ok Katherine?*", "*Yes, Yes I am fine, oh my god I am more than fine.*"

I was quickly adding figures up in my mind, we were both on £70 quid so £140, take the rent off this, and the bills, it would leave us with £5 to our name each week, would Craig agree?

My boss shouted over, "*Katherine*", "yes?", I switched the hairdryer back on, finished her hair with the biggest grin on my face, we could really do this, a house, a real house, our house, our first home.

Yes it was going to be tight, but we had love, and as the saying goes "LOVE IS ALL YOU NEED".

I hugged my client, which was very unusually I did not hug clients ha, but I was so excited. I said yes without even asking Craig, but it was too good, I had not even seen the house, the area. I was going with my gut, this was meant to happen, I was meant to do this ladies hair, whoop could not wait to finish work and tell Craig.

I could not text him, I did not have a phone, a mobile one that is, so it had to wait, but boy it would be so worth the wait. Craig was more excited than me when I told him.

We had both passed our driving tests too, but I did not have a car. My dad was a car salesman, still waiting for my first car I was promised, but that's another story.

Craig had bought himself a second hand mini, and over the weekends he would spend hours doing it up, it looked well smart. It was red with a black roof, matching wing mirrors and a walnut dash and big speakers and bucket seats, his pride and joy, apart from me that was ha ha.

We drove up to see the house before telling anyone.

It was all cream with a wooden door with the number 3 on it, it felt like home even when only looking through the tinted windows of the mini. We looked at each other and we just knew it was going to be ours.

Now for the big task of telling parents we were moving out, our own place to call home. We could not be happier.

Ok Craig's parents did not take it well at all, Craig's dad shouting "*he can't afford tools let alone move out*", they soon calmed down, and supported our decision.

My dad was fine about it, "*as long as you're happy my Katherine*", he would always say this, he had his own troubles in life again, something I will not be writing about, but he was dealt an unlucky card at times, with relationships.

I sit my mum down, "*Mum, Craig and I have got our on place to move into, we move in 4 weeks*". She looked a little confused, lit a cigarette and popped the kettle on, her usual routine. "*You will still have to pay me rent up until you move out!*"

Yup this was her first words, she was not bothered at all I thought, well I hoped she would be, strange I know, but I still craved that mum. I replied with glazed over eyes, trying to hold it all together, "*Do Not Worry You Will Get Your Money*".

I remember running upstairs wanting to be so happy, yet again feeling so let down.
Big girl pants needed!!! I gave my head a wobble and started to look around my room.

With so many sad memories here, I could not wait to be gone, I felt it was the only way for my actual life to start. A childhood forgotten, a fresh beginning.

It's moving day. We had borrowed a van off a friend, not a closed van an open one, ha ha. We looked like the Clampetts moving.

I had my nan's sofas out of my room, a rocking chair, a second hand cooker and washing machine. We had bought a new bed, it costs £99 with the headboard a lovely pink velvet one. It was like a board, but it was new, and it was ours.

We had the clothes on our back and a few items in a suitcase, 18 years packed into one van, the van that was going to take me from number 55, from my mum, from what had been forever, there was no going back, not now not ever.

Craig beeped the horn it was time to go, I turned to my mum, I wanted to be upset, I wanted her to be sad I was leaving, but there was nothing.

She lent in to hug me, my body would still freeze when this happened, a very uncomfortable feeling, not one of love but dread. I would do anything not to have affection with her, trying to push things to the back of my mind, but they were always there, the thought the memories.

Opening the squeaky gate, I look up and down the street, and gaze at the orange door of 55, with my mother, sitting on the step and smoking, memories all flash before me.

I turn to Craig, his big amazing excited smile, he was my future, I turned and walked to the van, getting in, popping my seat belt on, winding the window down to wave to my mum, but she had already gone in and closed the door.

Number 55 was in my past, here's to the future. We drove out of the street and onto to our new life in Bagillt, in our new home, just us.

That night once everything was sorted, Craig's parents surprised us with a new table and chairs and a bookcase, we were thrilled, to have brand new stuff was amazing.

What was more amazing is I felt relief, for the first time in my life. I felt a cloud lifting, I felt I had now a future, a happy one. My mum was still there, still in my life, but I did not feel anxiety, emotions of dread, I felt happy and in love, and excited what the future held for Katherine and Craig.

Chapter 12 - Becoming Mum

Two years had passed, we had made our little two up two down a home, hardly spending any time there, we worked so much.

We were still earning minimum wage at the age of 20 years, hairdressers did not get paid much I discovered, but I made extra money from tips.

Craig's wage had gone up, but he was traveling a lot to work, so all the spare extra money went on fuel and keeping the car on the road. We never missed a rent payment ever.

We would however press the emergency gas and electric button, this would then give us five pound extra, before we got paid again.

We were managing to pay the water rates and the council tax, TV licence, what we were not managing was to keep ourselves very well.

We would have five-pound left at the end of it all for food, we would eat Weetabix with water, or buy a Swiss roll for thirty pence and a packet of custard for twenty pence, just so it would fill us up, not ideal I know, but we were young and invincible remember and very much in love.

When I look back now I really do not know how we survived. Craig's parents would invite us down for Sunday lunch and for Christmas dinner.

I think this kept us going, we never told anyone of our struggles, because at the time they did not seem that bad, we had our home, a job, and each other and that is all that mattered.

We were both working so much that we did not have many visitors. Over the weekend we would be busy keeping up with washing, cleaning and doing the garden.

We kind of lost our way, too busy making a living to actually have a life. Something needed to change.

I could not physically work more hours, and neither could Craig. So, I decided, to go on a night course to learn Child development, something that had interested me for a while.

Maybe the urge to see how a child should be cared for and brought up I do not know, but I finished my course while in the salon.

Working in the day, to then go to night school. I got another qualification of childcare NVQ level 2, this meant I could seek a new career with children as a nursery nurse.

Unfortunately, the pay also was not as good, long hours, but more potential. In the salon, unless I owned it there was nowhere else for me to further my career in this, no chance of a pay rise or a promotion, I was just stuck.

So with that I handed in my notice, because I had got myself a job in the local Day Nursery, looking after children from 6 weeks old to school age of five.

It was hard work, but a new group of friends and I loved my job, seeing all the little faces of the children, playing, feeding, reading taking care of them. It was then I knew I wanted to become a mum.

Before this I thought I never would, so scared to bring a life into the world. What if I suffer with my mental health, what if the baby does, who would help me, be my role model to be the best mum? All these questions I had, and I had no answers to them.

Craig and I were solid, so in love and content, he was the man I wanted to grow old with, he was the man I wanted to be the father of my children.

After a long arse day in work, Craig came home, covered in dust like always from working, I ran him a bath. We had no central heating in the house, only a fire in the lounge, a gas one, so we did not use it much to save money. But what we would do is have a hot bath together to get all warm and cosy, before popping on 15 layers in the winter. It was a cold, cold house, and money was tight.

Evenings in the bath we would put the world to rights as they say, and have big heart to heart. This was the evening I would say how I wanted us to have a baby, yep crazy, we were living off Weetabix and water, and now I wanted a baby.

I put it in around about way not knowing his answer, we had never spoke about children before. I said, *"Craig would you want a family or to get married first?"*. His reply *"Well, I would love to get married but we just cannot afford it, so I would say kids would come first"*.

I was thrilled with his answer, writing this is so crazy listening to the words back, we cannot afford a wedding but thought a baby would be cheaper, how young and naive we were hey?

I splashed him in the face with the now lukewarm water and said "*so that's it then shall we try for a baby?*" and that was it, from that day forward we were going to try and become parents.

We told no one, except my sister. I was so close to her and respected her and loved her dearly, she was my best friend. She had a child my beautiful niece, I would help out with her a lot while my sister went out to work.

People thought she was mine at times, I felt proud to think of her like that, my sister then went on to have another gorgeous girl, so I was very lucky to have them in my life. She would give me advice on what I needed to do, first stop a visit to the GP.

I had been on the contraceptive pill since I was 14, due to suffering with heavy periods, and stomach cramps. Six years was a long time, so my sister said I best get it checked.

The doctor said it is a myth that the pill needs to come out of your system, but he went onto to say, I was underweight, which I knew, and still anaemic, so he said come off the pill and start on some folic acid, this will give you the best start to becoming a mum.

I started to really look after myself, eating my greens, taking my supplements, building myself up to be a mum. Buying every magazine I could when I could afford it, reading about everything and taking advice off my sister.

If I was doing this then I was doing it to the best of my ability. Most young girls, would go to their mum for advice, but I did not have this option, I did not want my Mum to know at all.

We had been trying for 1 month, the day had come, my period was due, and yup there it was my period, I thought oh well it can't happen that quick, 2nd month 3rd month 4th month, still nothing. I was devastated, could I not have children? Could Craig not have Children? I would be heartbroken, if I could not make a baby.

Month 5, 3 days late, 1 week late, starting to grin, but not wanting to get my hopes up, my sister said find an empty bottle and we will take it to the chemist.

Yes, years ago, you did not pee on a stick, you took your urine to the chemist, waited in the queue then on a piece of paper they wrote your result.

I waited in line, handed my pee over, and waited some more, my sister popping her arm around me as she had done many times before growing up.

They were safe arms, I looked at her, I felt upset, even before I knew the outcome, just looking at her and what she had been through, what her eyes, body had seen, felt, there she was this strong female, fierce, helping me as always, I loved her with all my heart.

Miss Ferneyhough, I heard my name called, she handed a folded piece of paper, we walked over to the corner of the chemist and I slowly opened the paper from each corner. There it was in black and white, POSITIVE.... I was about to become a mum, I burst into uncontrollable tears, and my sister did too, her baby sister was going to be a mum, who would of thought?

Back at home now, waiting eagerly for Craig's return. I kept getting up to look out of the window to see his mini come up the street. I felt like the time just dragged.

I walked over to the full length mirror in our bathroom, looked at myself up and down turning to the side and stroking my tummy.

Glancing at myself again in the mirror, looking myself in the eyes, and talking to myself. "*You're going to be a mum, you're actually making a life inside you*".

This moment I still have so clear in my mind, the moment of excitement and dread. Would I be ok? could I do this? I hear the door open, it's Craig, I hold back, still in the bathroom. I have been waiting to tell him all day and now I have a nervous belly. He is going to be a Dad something we both wanted so much, what was I waiting for?

"*Craig sit down*", he turned to me and came over held me in his arms holding the back of my head as I gazed into his eyes, he said "*your pregnant?*", "*Yes, Yes*" I shouted, "*We are having a baby*".

We both could not quite believe it, he knew how I was feeling because now it was time to tell my mum and dad and of course Craig's parents.

We drove to number 55 first. This house was feeling so different now. You know when you move out and it all just seems so different, you couldn't even imagine living there or even had lived there.

Strange feeling. I still had a front door key for emergencies with my mum. I let myself in and walked into the kitchen.

The smell overpowered me of smoke, so strong, stronger than I could remember when I lived there, it took my breath and I started to cough. My mum was in her usual chair, re lighting her roley that had just gone out, her boyfriend also smoking, and of course drinking tea.

I told them my news, it was so odd, because she said congratulations, but then went on to say she was going to try for another baby. It was like she was not pleased really and wanted it to be about her.

Baby I thought, my mother could not have another child, she had already had four children but eight pregnancies. She was getting older and her health was not great let alone her mental health.

I knew she would want to give the man she was with a child, he had no children. I really did not know what to say, other than scream at her and shout *"are you fucking JOKING!!"*.

But I kept it in, I was carrying my unborn baby, I did not want to get stressed out or have anything happen, so I said I did not think it was a good idea, but up to you, I then left.

Getting in the car, I could feel I was so angry inside. I had just told her I was going to be a first time mum, this was a big deal, it was her grandchild, but all she could think of was making another child with a man with a severe Mental Health illness, and herself the same.

No child should be brought into this world to then in their adulthood try and recover from their childhood. It was selfish and very unfair. I tried to calm down as we drove to Craig's parents to tell them our exciting news, we were hoping they would be a little bit more excited.

I could see how nervous Craig was. For his parents this would be their first grandchild, their first son to have a baby, this was a big thing.

Deep breath in as we entered the house. It did not go like the fairy tale I had hoped for. No one congratulating us, no one wrapping their arms around us with excitement, the look of fear on Craig's mum's face.

Craig's dad was in the bath, his mum headed up stairs to break the news.

We heard a bang and a splash while his dad shouted "*He cannot afford tools for work let alone a baby*".

We quickly made our way home in silence. This amazing news of a life did not seem to be everyone's amazing news. Craig's parents were just worried, but Craig and I knew It all....right?

The main thing was we were over the moon to become parents. Yes, we would struggle, it would be hard, but we had planned this. It was no accident, we had been trying for months and now it was a reality, our baby, growing inside me.

I thought to myself, yes we haven't got a lot but what we did have was each other and enough love inside us both to give this baby the best life.

Maybe not the materialistic things but I did not see that of importance at all, all I saw was my upbringing, and I knew it was not just about me now, so I will do anything and everything I can to give this baby the most stable, loving environment I could. Craig would be the perfect dad, I just knew it.

My dad took the news like he did all news, in his stride, congratulating us. I felt so distant from him, but again I needed to work on me now and that not only meant my body and looking after that, it also meant my mind.

This to me was the most important thing. I did not want to be like my mum, I would tell myself this over and over just, so I believed it. I was so scared deep down.

Could I love this child I would ask myself? when I find it hard to be loved and have so many insecurities. Then I would shake myself and know that this baby was a gift, a gift to me to create a whole new life as a mother myself.

My body changed so quickly. Being 7 stone I quickly noticed the weight I was gaining. For the first time I looked healthy, I even had a slight bust which was a first for me. I would talk to my unborn baby, telling it how much I loved it, we did not know the sex of the child we wanted it to be a surprise.

Craig was working harder than ever, doing weekends to earn extra cash, I was still in the nursery doing 50 hours a week, as well as baby sitting in the evening for clients of the nursery for extra cash.

One of my clients was selling her pram, it was navy blue with big flowers on, big hood and a basket, underneath, she wanted £100 pound for it, we knew we needed a pram, just did not have the hundred pound.

Craig played guitar, and had made himself a guitar case, out of wood, his pride and joy, but guess what? I was carrying his pride and joy, so with that he surprised me by selling it all, then used the money to buy the pram, we were over the moon.

Craig's parents, after two whole weeks of not talking to us, finally came around. They said how worried they were but were here and excited just nervous. That made us feel so much better. They had come up with so much stuff for the baby, a bath, Moses basket, a box full of toiletries and nappies, we were over the moon, such a huge help.

What shocked me the most was my mother came around to the house and she had bought Craig and I a present. I could not believe my eyes she had only gone and bought me a brand-new cot.

I do not know where she got the money from, I did not ask, I was made up with the gift. This was a massive thing for my mum to do, huge, we just did not buy presents like this.

I wanted to hug her, but still at 20 years again my body would stop me and freeze. She would come over to hug me and kiss me, and still I would crawl inside. Would these feeling ever go? would they get worse once I had my own child? It freaked me out to even think about it.

Nine months passed so fast, I felt I had such a short pregnancy. I worked up until 2 weeks before having my baby. I was overdue now by 10 ten days and gained four stone. I felt like a whale, the biggest I had ever been in my entire life.

Craig had just been the best, making me still feel attractive and wanted. He would rub my belly and chat to it and we would look at each other with so much excitement. Everything was ready, the nursery, my hospital bag, we just needed baby to make an appearance.

Craig went to work early that morning, I ran myself a bath, it was the month of September, September the 11th.

While lying in the bath I began to feel unwell, I sat up, and I knew I was in labour. I rang Craig straight away, by the time he arrived home my contractions were thick and fast, grabbing hold of him with the pain, his face was a picture. Quickly getting into the car and driving to the hospital.

I was having very strong contractions now and wanted to push. The midwife said I was ready.

After pushing for so long I needed some help, while just on gas and air and Craig too ha ha. I just wanted the baby out now, you know that feeling if I have any mums reading this, your exhausted, excited, cannot go on anymore, yup that feeling!

The doctor came in and popped my legs into stirrups, the baby's heart rate had dropped he needed to get the baby out. I thought Craig was going to pass out, but he held my hand so tight and stroked my head. The doctor then made his cut and used a vontose cap, to suck the baby out.

Within seconds of that they placed a very blue baby onto my tummy by my chest before taking the baby away quickly. I was terrified, was my baby ok? there was no cry.

Craig and I were just looking at each other, I was even too scared to cry myself, just holding each other, we waited, and waited.

There it was that cry we all wait for, they wrapped the baby up and handed it to me. The relief over took us both and we were now in tears both of us.

Congratulations on your son Mr Massey, he is 8lb and 3ozs…..OMG we had a son.

My legs still in mid air while the doctor was stitching me up, I did not care, here I held my child, my son Harry George Massey. We had created a life and in that very moment I looked at him, I loved him more than life.

I was overwhelmed by him, I brought his pink screwed up face to my face and kissed him. The feeling I felt, was utter love. It was not me or Craig now it was him my beautiful son. Once a broken little girl myself, now a mother, and I was going to do the best I could by him.

Chapter 13 - All too much

Time to leave the hospital with our son. Walking down the corridor so proud looking at Craig carrying him and my bag. I could hardly walk, stitched from back to front, wearing my jeans, yup jeans!!

No one told me you do not go straight back to your normal size. No one told me I would be picking my tummy up off the floor and popping it into my pants while trying to walk with stitches.

And oh my god, why did no one tell me about when your milk comes in? and then you start your period!! Are you actually fecking joking, I was a mess. All these things aside I was besotted by my son, our son, so much love for him.

We walked to the car, our little mini. We looked at the car seat we had bought and yep it would not fit. The car was so small, we were never going to fit a pram in the boot. I climbed into the back seat best I could.

Craig passing me Harry, we knew then that another thing needed to go, we now would need a family car. I thought Craig would be so sad to see his mini go but to my surprise becoming a dad made him grow up a lot.

Not that he was happy buying a Maestro ha ha...but it's all we could afford, it felt like driving a bus, but it is what we all needed.

Bringing Harry home to our little house. We were now a family, I felt so blessed to have him.

It was time for visitors. All the family came from Craig's side, his parents were over the moon with a grandson, Craig is one of three boys, so they were used to boys.

My dad was chuffed to have a grandson but busy with his own life, working hard and his own difficulties that I will not write about and a nine year old son, my baby brother.

Time for My Mum to meet him. She had one son of her own that was estranged from her, but she still thought so much of him, she loved boys.

She picked Harry up out of his Moses basket, again my body was so tense more so now. I had this overwhelming feeling to protect him, to keep him safe. You should not have those thoughts when your own mother is holding her grandchild, but I did, and those feelings got stronger and stronger.

Naming him Harry after my Grandad, I had never met, but a man my mum spoke so highly of, a man that was safe, that made her safe that was taken too soon.

She was made up by this, I hoped it would bring us closer, that we would now do the mother, daughter, grand kid things. Walk to the park, play football, bake cakes, my imagination unfortunately was just that, these things never happen.

I would have called Harry Tom after my other granddad, but that name had been given to my baby brother in memory of my granddad, my dad's dad.

Another great man taken from us. Why were all the good men taken so soon? I was to make sure that my little man would be one of them, a good man with a heart full of love, a gentleman. It was in my heart to do my best no matter what role models I had around me.

I had my memories of Grandma's house, she would become my role model. I remembered lots of things from her, and with Craig's Parents too, and my sister. Harry would have the best people around him.

You did not have maternity pay back then, so after 2 very short weeks I returned back to work, still bruised and swollen, sore boobs, and a new-born in tow, there was no other choice, we needed the money more than ever now.

My boss had given me the position of looking after the babies in the baby unit, 5 new born babies, and of course my own son who I was allowed to bring with me free of charge. At the time I thought this would be the best thing, no child care costs, no relying on anyone to look after Harry and still earning money, win, win, or so I thought.

Harry would be there crying, his eyes out while I fed and looked after the other babies, changing them and settling them, so my work friends did not think I was favouring Harry, but what I was doing was neglecting my sons needs.

I would go home after a very long 10 hours, remove my wet pads where my milk had leaked out when Harry cried, it was drying up. I did try breastfeeding but knew I could not continue because of work, and yes back then getting your boob out had more stigma. My picture in my head of motherhood was far from what my reality was.

Up in the night doing all the feeds, because Craig had work too and had to drive then do a very physical Job. Yes he should of helped more but I felt myself not wanting his help to the point of pushing him away. Neglecting our relationship, and only focusing on being a mum, that's all that mattered.

I was shattered, not healed from birth, and wanting to prove to everyone I was super mum, I could hold down a full-time job while bringing Harry up, running a house, and being a girlfriend. The reality was I was doing none of this right. I was at breaking point.

Crying most nights to myself in the bath this is not what I pictured it to be like. My body had changed, my mind was doing over time.

Craig and I were going further and further apart just existing in the same house, being mum and dad but that was it. What had happened to us? was this it? Was this what life would be like?

I could not take anymore. I held my baby boy in my arms and sobbed. I was letting him down, I was lost, I never asked for help just kept pushing myself and pushing myself until I broke.

Craig said "*You need to see someone, a doctor, you're not yourself, this can't go on*". All I needed was some help, but I would not ask.

I sat in the waiting room of the doctors with Harry in his pram, rocking him back and forth. He was a very sickly baby, projectile vomiting all the time.

I thought it was normal, people saying I was not winding him right. I felt a failure as a mother and Harry was only 6 weeks old, I knew I loved him, wanted him, what was wrong with me?

The doctor called my name, he chatted for a while and then wrote on a piece of paper a prescription. I thought what tablets are going to make me become a better mum? then I read the name, I just stared at the paper, and went numb.

Anti-depression tablets, the same tablets I would lay out on the kitchen top for my mother, why was he giving me these? "*Katherine you have post natal depression*". I did not know what this was, but I knew what these tablets were, I knew how addictive they were, I thanked the doctor and left.

At home I settled Harry after he had been very sick again. Reaching into my bag and looking at the tablets, then glancing at Harry in his crib. I cried some more.

I began to think back to my childhood, having flashes of different things. I walked over and picked Harry out of his crib and just lay with him rocking him, sobbing my heart out.

It was that moment, I got up and threw the tablets in the bin, stroking Harry's face and telling him I can do this, and I will son, I promise not to let you down, and I won't.

With that, I opened up to Craig, and he understood, completely. We felt so close again, we had lost our way, I knew what we needed to do. I rang work and handed my notice in, I do not know what we were thinking financially but what I did know was, for me to work on me. I needed all my focus at home with my son.

Life was going to get a whole lot tougher, but I knew I had made a promise not only to me but to my child. I promised him to be the best mum I could, and from that day forward I took charge of my life. Not saying I did not have bad days, I still do, but I learnt to work on me, my mind set, in return, this helped us as a family.

Harry still being sick, I took him to the doctor, again him saying it's normal some babies are just sicker than others.

Not happy with his answer I took him to hospital with Craig. A lovely doctor, examined him, not a peep out of him such a good baby. Then my world yet again came crashing down, he said he had a heart murmur, and would need a scan and x-ray to further investigate.

What did this even mean? I felt so guilty, going back to work too soon, was it my fault. I was reassured that this happened in the womb and was not found until today.

The worst news ever was that my son had a hole in his heart and stomach, hence the sick. I imagined the worst open-heart surgery. My heart sank, this baby so precious, so good and yet so poorly. Thank god I used my motherly instincts and took him for a second opinion.

The good news was that the hole was that small they said in some cases it can close itself, and the stomach one would heal with 6 months once sitting up. We were left with our thoughts and a whole load of paperwork on the next steps.

Yes, you guessed it. It broke my heart, Craig holding me close, awfully upset himself. He had a girlfriend who was nearly losing it and now a poorly son, and he was the only one bringing an income in. The pressure was on, but our only main concern was Harry.

Harry went from strength to strength, proving all the professionals wrong. He started talking at 6 months and sitting up, his sickness had nearly gone. We still needed 20 bibs and 10 changes of clothes, but we had progress.

I went back to my roots and started to do hairdressing again, mobile. When Craig came home from work I would go out. Not ideal but it meant another wage and it took some pressure off. Craig was earning more now, too. He was making us all proud, being the best dad, provider, and also my best friend and lover.

I also started doing the Avon and Kleeneze, another thing I could do around having a baby. I even tried being a van driver and delivering parcels, but I only lasted a day at this. God loves a trier, right?

Life was ok. We had more money, Harry's health was improving, mine was a million miles from where it had been. Life gets tough, the tough get going as they say, and that's exactly what we did.

Time went on and we were at a stage that we could afford a mortgage. Yes, I could not believe it either. From Weetabix and water to owning a house. My beautiful Grandma had passed leaving me some money and this helped us with a deposit for our next home.

Without that help we could never have done it, I still thank her today. Part of me wanted to blow it, haha, but I knew if we wanted to move forward with our future that these were the next steps. I never had that kind of money given to me ever, I was so grateful and still am today. I am grateful that even on her passing she looked out for me, looking after me as she always did. I miss her so, so much.

We are now in our very first own home. Time passed. I have wrote this poem for you to fill in the gaps.

Age 11 Craig saw me and thought he had gone to heaven,
One look one glance started our childhood romance,

By age 14 still going strong, but something had gone terribly wrong,
Craig had grown his hair as long as mine,
Big black boots, mac and a Guns N Roses sign,
Well they say love is blind
Years passed so very fast we were older, wiser with a bit more cash,
We started as two but then we grew, now we were four and back to being poor,
I look back in time It's clear for me to see, that I was meant for you, and you were meant for me,

All the fun and games, and what we have
right now really has not changed,
This brings my poem to an end
That I found life and love with my best
friend.

I wrote that poem for our wedding day. Yes,
we were now married, and we were a family
of four.

Craig said *"Shall we give Harry a brother or
Sister?"*

I could not believe what I was hearing. I
longed so much for family of my own but
was so scared by the reality of it.

What If I get poorly again, what If I cannot
love another child the way I love Harry?
What if another baby was sick? Could we
even afford another child?

All of these questions I had. After talking
everything through, we did try for a baby.
The most precious second gift was given to
me, my beautiful baby girl, my gorgeous
Olivia.

My beautiful daughter born with long dark
hair and blue eyes, the image of her dad.
She not only completed us as a family, she
completed me as a Mother, my girl. I was
about to become the mum I knew I could be.

I was in a really good place, two children, a husband and we owned our home. Life was going well, we were becoming more secure. The one thing that was not going well, that held me back all the time, was my Mother.

I was blessed with two beautiful children and now both were happy and healthy. I was trying hard every day to be the mum that I always wanted my mum to be.

However, there were always my thoughts, my deepest thoughts that would not leave me. I wanted to protect my children. I can't explain the way I felt, but the emotion that overtook me to keep my children safe became an obsession.

I was full time mum, not leaving them with anyone. Wanting the best for them as most mums do.

Craig's parents were fab grandparents and still are. They had so much love and security around them, just as I wanted it, but I still worried about my mum's mental state. I worried so much about her effect around the children growing up.

I had so many different men/dads in my life. I did not want the same for my two, I did not want them seeing different people in and out of their lives and I did not want them seeing me upset with my mother's actions. They were getting older and noticing more and more.

When I knew my mum was visiting, my whole day would change I would get anxious and start snapping at Craig and my children.

It was the dread. It was never a happy visit, just one about how awful her life was or the dramas in it. Growing up, I tried and tried to understand but now it was about my kids, they were to come first.

The things that happened next made me make a life changing decision.

Chapter 14 - Judgement and Grief

Life is better with your best friend, that's why I married mine.

Friends. What is the meaning of friends?

I suppose it's different for everyone. My friends became my family to make up for the lack of having actual family around.
We start making friends in school, and for some we are lucky enough to have them as friends for life.

Growing up, your circle of friendships grow. School friends, work friends, hobby friends and now, of course, the book of face friends. I broke the word up.

Friendship. I think of friendships as exactly this, imagine one big ship with all of your friends on filled to the top like a cruise liner. Some stay on the ship because they totally get your friendship and you.

The friends that stick on the ship are the ones that know about the bumps and waves along the way of life, but they also see the wonderful calm and fun times, so they stick around.

Some jump overboard at the first hurdle, they cannot cope with the truth, they do not like to see you doing well. These were not friends in the first place, they were life lessons and just passing through the port!

Some stay on the ship, but get off at different ports, and visit the ship from time to time. Then there are the friendships that sailed on your ship and it just sank. You wonder what might have happened, what went so wrong that they did not want a ticket aboard your ship anymore.

That's how I look at friendships. One thing that happened to me and still does is getting judged by people even when they do not even know you, your background or your story.

From a very early age this would happen. You see that girl there, that little girl. She is the one with the mad mum.

You see that girl there with the long hair? You know the one, the nitty kid with the mental mum. She's got loads of dads her, wonder if she knows which is which.

Onto high school. Look at her with her crooked teeth, greasy hair and spotty skin. What the hell is she wearing? She has not even got any boobs, like an ironing board. She looks like a boy! What make are her trainers, she's a gypo.

When I reached adulthood and we started to do ok, becoming more secure, owning our own house, business, and driving a nice car, "*Who does she think she is? Stuck up cow*" and
"*Up her own arse that one.*"

No matter what I did, I was always judged. Losing friends along the way, no one truly ever knowing me or my story. My walls grew higher, my skin grew thicker, and I was becoming stronger. All of this torment was turning me into who I am today.

The judgemental women, the ones that looked, pointed the finger and laughed. Shame on you. I have had to stay strong for my children and to stay strong to know my story was not over yet.

So, let's get back to the story. My story, my true life story.

I did not leave my children often. When I did, it would only be with Craig's parents. I could trust them.

We had another family funeral coming up. My children were too young to come and the only person I could leave them with would be my mother.

I paced for days over this, Craig reassuring me that it would only be a few hours they will be fine, so that was it. I dropped the children off with my mum, their nana. They would be safe, right?

My mum was now with another man. Yep, another one. He made me feel very uncomfortable, looked me up and down.

Just made me cringe, but I did have trust issues. Every man made me feel like this. I would think every man except Craig had a motive.

I returned to pick my children up. I have never drove so fast after the funeral. I was alone, everyone was at the wake. I was going to take the children back there.

It was Craig's side of the family, hence not having anyone to look after my children. I keep saying 'my' instead of 'our', it's so you do not get lost in my words. I write with emotion and sometimes this can be confusing. I know, keep up.

Remember, I still have a key for 55 so no need to knock. I place the key into the rusty door. There was a nack, to use this it never left me. I closed the door quietly and walked up the hall to hear the words *"Shut the fuck up, you little bitch,"* then my daughters cries.

I rush into the kitchen and there was the strange man, squeezing my daughters hand. I quickly grabbed her into my arms, reassuring her. I was looking for Harry. I glanced up and there he was in the garden with my mum.

Just as I was about to go outside, this happened so quickly. Harry stood on my mum's plants, her flower beds, her pride and joy garden. She shouted so loud at him and slapped his legs so hard he fell to the ground. There he lay on the path, crying.

I ran to him, Olivia already upset in my arms and resting on my hip. I found the strength to scoop Harry up and pop him on my other hip, looking my mother directly in the eye. I said *"You will never, never have your grandchildren again!"*

More images flashing before me, too many times of being smacked myself, my sisters and brother. The cycle was continuing.

The thing was that my mother thought it was ok. I rushed them to the wake and told Craig. I knew they were safe now, and I flew back to number 55.

On my return the man said *"She was making too much noise, I wanted to read my paper"*. My mother said *"Harry should know better not to stand on flowers"*.

I was horrified. Why did I let them stay there? Thank God it was not for any longer. I told my mum I wanted to speak with her once I had calmed down. I needed to tell her exactly how I felt once and for all.

That conversation took me four more years to make. I cannot explain why it took that long. She had, like, this hold on me where I would not forgive, but I would try understand her illness, and cling on to the fact that I just wanted a mum but this could not go on.

Things were getting worse. Every time she went near them, every time she went near me, I would shake, sweat, and not be in a good place at all.

I think all the people around me would say "*Your Mum is so nice*". It would stop me in my tracks. I would want to scream "*NO, she's fucking not,*" but instead I would nod and smile while crying inside with the truth. You all know that saying you only get one mum, right?

I had to make a decision and I had to make one now or never. Guess what? The man that squashed Olivia's hand and told her to shut the fuck up, he had now gone. Yup, there was now another man.

She was madly in love with him and about to marry him. I know, I cannot believe it either and it was my fucking real life!

She said the kids can call him Grandad. I heard this so many times while growing up, "*You can call him dad, Katherine*". So many men, so much traffic through the home. Like Hell were my kids calling him Grandad. They had two grandads and that's all they needed.

My mind was made up. I sat my mum down in the kitchen in her usual chair, watched her light a fag and drink a cup of tea. I asked her the question I wanted to ask so many years ago, "*Mum, did you really lose your memory with your treatment*"?

My body is still, my eyes glazed and fixed on hers. She exhales her smoke, leans over, blows the smoke directly into my face, and says "*NO, I remember everything, Katherine*".

This said with a little laugh a smirk as she takes another deep breath of smoke and blows it up to the kitchen ceiling.

"*I saved you, Katherine, I saved you,*" these were the words that haunt my soul to this very day. Even writing them, tears fill my eyes.

"*Saved me from what, mum? Saved me from what?*" I said it calmly, like I already knew the answer.

"*From that man. It was me that stopped that, Katherine, me*", it was like she wanted to be congratulated, to be given the mum of the year award.

She remembered everything she told me right there. It made me sick. If she remembered everything, then she knew about the abuse. Not only to me, but to my siblings, worse for them.

I had tried so hard for years and years to put it all behind me and to keep striving for a mother and daughter relationship, battling with my physical and mental health, holding it all together to be given yet another kick in the teeth.

When would this nightmare end, when would I wake up without the feeling of dread? I could not go on.

I went home and broke down to Craig. I broke down one too many times. He was my rock, but I wanted to be the best mum, the best wife, and I was being held back.

I knew I could not have my mother in my life anymore. How would I tell her? I looked over at my children. I had put them at risk. This was not going to happen again.

My decision was made. Craig has asked me if I was absolutely positive. I was. I could only become who I wanted to be without the constant reminder of what was or what was still.

The cycle of male traffic had to stop, my kids needed a stable upbringing with a mother who had a stable mind. I knew it was right but it was going to be so, so hard.

Would she get what I was about to say to her, that I would never see her again? Would that sink into her fragile mind? I would only know if I did it, but what happened next turned my world upside down.

My Mother did not get it at all, telling me to go away, calm down and come see her when I knew what I was talking about. With the mental illness that my mum had, the whole world revolved around what was in her mind and in her world.

If she did not want to hear something, she wouldn't. She would just blank it, stare past you and talk about what she wanted to talk about.

Weeks went by, the message slowly sinking in. Children's birthdays and Christmas, Easter. I would send the presents, cards and eggs back to number 55. I wanted nothing more to do with her.

That evening there was a knock at the door. It was my mother screaming for me to let her in, to let her see her grandchildren.

Funny, she never did say she wanted to see me, just the grandchildren. I quickly whisked the kids away upstairs and asked Craig to tell her to go.

I heard him say "*She does not want to see you anymore, so that means you won't see our children either, please go now,*".

Still screaming that they were her grandchildren. I just sat at the top of the stairs holding my children and keeping them safe while feeling so upset inside. Yes, this was my decision, but it was still so, so hard.

Eventually, she went. I watched her walk up the street, not turning around once. That would be the last that I saw of my Mother.

Was I now to have the peace I always wanted, the fresh start, just Craig and I with our children for the future?

I was not close to my eldest sister, she had moved away while I was young and only visited now and then when it suited. She had one child, my niece.

It was a Sunday afternoon, the phone rang, it was my niece asking if I would go and see my sister. The thing was she was at mum's house, my niece said it's very important. So with that I made my way down to 55 not knowing what to expect. I was on my own while Craig watched our children at home.

I pulled outside just gazing at the door not thinking I would ever step foot in there again, but it was a strange call off my sister, so I wanted to know what was wrong.

Funny enough I still had my key, Mum never asked for it back. So here I am again at the door of 55, turning the key like so many times before and not knowing what lay behind it. What was going to be said that needed me to urgently to go down?

Walking down the hall once again, turning the handle of the kitchen door, there stood my eldest sister in the kitchen by herself. I could see mum, her now husband and my niece in the garden from the kitchen window. What was so important you needed me to come straight down?

My sister was angry, never seen her like this with me before, I just let her speak and said nothing back. Going on and on about me not speaking to Mum and how wrong I was.

"*Katherine you know what we have all been through but we all choose to still have Mum In our lives*". I tried to explain to her how I was feeling, and for my decision that did not happen overnight.

She was not listening, just going on and on getting more and more angry, I could tell she had been drinking too.

We were still alone in the kitchen, "*Katherine you have had a good life, a great life compared to what we had. You had a TV In your room and nan's sofa, you were the golden child, the untouched one*".

Remembering that I had not shared anything with my siblings about my time at home with mum, she still was shouting, then all of a sudden went calm, she leaned against the kitchen table and looked over at me, my back up against the kitchen door, with my hand on the handle wanting to escape.

"*Katherine, how do you know that I am not your Mum?*" She kept talking and talking, but I could not hear her words, I was focused on her lips, but could not hear the words coming out all I could hear was "*She could be my Mum*".

My head was in complete shock, I grabbed the handle of the door turning it and ran out of the door and into my car, I was not followed.

Running into my garden sobbing, Craig shouting what has happen Katherine, what has happened?

My words would not come out, just more and more tears.

Was my whole life a lie. Was the women I called Mum now my Nan? Did that mean my dad was not my dad? did that mean my dad had a relationship with my sister? Why did my sister not take me with her? Why was I with Mum? Was this the real reason behind the Golden Child?

Craig calmed me down and said "*Do Not believe a word of it, it's all messed up and your better off out of it*".

I knew he was right. I bet you're thinking I went to seek the truth behind what I was told? the answer is no. For the first time in my life I had been woken up, what was real or not, I did not care.

What I cared about was my children and my husband, and from that day forward I moved forward with my life. Slowly but surely, little by little, finding myself, dropping the title of The Golden Child, The child with the mad mum. I was finding myself, becoming the person I knew was there with no one holding me back.

Finding Myself Again

I hope this helps anyone reading this, much love.

Stress, worry and anxiety simply come from projecting your thoughts into the future and imagining something bad. This is focusing on what you do not want!

If you find your mind projecting into the future in a negative way, focus intensely on the NOW! Keep bringing yourself back to the present.

Use all your focus and will, because in this moment of now there is utter peace.

I share these words with you, because this is exactly what I have had to do.

I work on myself a little each day, do I have bad days?

Hell yes!...Days where I cannot think straight, dark deep times, that still affect me deeply. But I am a survivor not a victim of my situation.

Yes, my Mental Health needs to be worked on every single day, but there was light at the end of that tunnel, I just lit the match myself.

I soon realised I could not live in a world without love.

My decision was made with integrity and truth. My writing these words of this my memoirs it's only now I can heal, because I have been vulnerable, and opened up.

I waited for my children to be old enough, for me to leave them my legacy, to reach for the stars, no matter what shit life throws your way.

I stayed strong for them and to write my story, to lay down my pen, to know someone found my words. To go on to help the future generations lead their best lives, with a healthy mind.

My work will continue with this as my passion in life, to bring an understanding to this Illness, we call Mental Health.

Printed in Great Britain
by Amazon

87813055R00119